Poetry from *Sojourner*

Poetry from
Sojourner

A Feminist Anthology

Edited by

Ruth Lepson with Lynne Yamaguchi

Introduction by

Mary Loeffelholz

University of Illinois Press

Urbana and Chicago

Library of Congress Cataloging-in-Publication Data
Poetry from Sojourner: a feminist anthology /
edited by Ruth Lepson with Lynne Yamaguchi ;
introduction by Mary Loeffelholz.
p.   cm.
Includes index.
ISBN 0-252-02885-6 (cl. : alk. paper)
ISBN 0-252-07154-9 (pbk. : alk. paper)
1. Feminist poetry, American. 2. American poetry—Women authors.
3. American poetry—20th century. 4. Women—Poetry. I. Lepson, Ruth.
II. Fletcher, Lynne Yamaguchi.
PS595.F45P64   2004
811'.540809287—dc21   2003007103

For Denise Levertov,

    who read us the poem as "onomatopoeia of experience,"

for Adrienne Rich,

    who gave us the essentials,

and for my mother.

    —R.L.

Contents

Preface

Ruth Lepson

Surprisingly, this collection is a first, an overview—as in review or historical survey. You can find other kinds of feminist poetry anthologies, but this one covers the range of writers in a feminist magazine during the period of feminism that coincides roughly with the quarter century during which *Sojourner* has existed.

Some of this anthology's poems differ in subject matter from those found in literary magazines. Although the poems aren't collocated by subject, subjects and attitudes recur that were nearly invisible in literary periodicals during this wave of feminism from 1975 on. The poets, editors, and readers of *Sojourner* developed a community and a forum that allowed for a more inclusive understanding of women's lives. And readership determines a great deal.

Lynne Yamaguchi and I, former poetry editors at the magazine, chose a small number of poems from among the twelve hundred or so that have appeared in *Sojourner,* our first consideration being quality. During my time as poetry editor, I had asked innovative poets to send their work, believing that radical experiments with language are feminist by nature, and I am especially happy to include some of those poems here. As Lyn Hejinian wrote in a letter of September 1993, "Poetry is a field of thought and information, and new modes of writing it provide not just new thoughts but also whole new ways of thinking."

There seems to be less of a sense of a women's community today than in, say, the 1960s and 1970s, and some younger women are reluctant to call themselves feminists because they fear marginalization or they imagine there is no need to do so. Gender issues remain largely invisible, but here, we hope, they are visible.

❲ ❲ ❲

We would like to thank *Sojourner*'s poetry editors, who chose the poems for the magazine: Kathleen Aguero, Jane Carter, Eli Clare, Liz Fenton, Miriam Goodman, Dorinda Hale, Ruth Lepson, Rosario Morales, Allison Platt (editor), Sarah Putman, Emily Skoler, Beverlyjean Smith, Shane Snowdon (managing editor), Lee Varon, Susan Wilson, Lynn Yamaguchi, and Laura Zimmerman.

And thanks to Linda Wong, Karen Kahn, and the interns at *Sojourner*, as well as Maureen Scully of *Sojourner*'s board.

And thanks a thousand times to Nina Nyhart, who, without prompting, subsidized much of the practical work of the anthology.

And to Louisa Solano of the Grolier Book Shop in Cambridge, Massachusetts, for suggesting the University of Illinois Press.

Many thanks to the assistants who worked on the anthology, friends and colleagues without whom this book would not exist: Irene Fairley, Mikhail Gershovich, Claudia Heiman, Edel Kehoe, Stephanie Koufman, Brian McGuire, Jennie Morris, Sue Pilaud, and Diane Putnam.

Introduction

Mary Loeffelholz

Fall 2000 marked the twenty-fifth anniversary of *Sojourner,* the Boston area's long-established feminist newspaper. From its founding, *Sojourner* has been a notable outlet for women's poetry; readers of *Sojourner* are accustomed to opening its pages every month to poems by authors from all walks of life, some of them famous, others seeing their poetry in print for the first time. Over the years *Sojourner* has published poems by some of the most honored names in American letters. The list of *Sojourner*'s contributors includes poets whose work has at one time or another earned them every major prize awarded in American poetry: Rita Dove, former Poet Laureate of the United States and winner of the Pulitzer Prize; Adrienne Rich, whose career began with the Yale Series of Younger Poets Award and who has since received the National Book Award, two Guggenheim Fellowships, a MacArthur Foundation Award, and the Shelley Memorial Award of the Poetry Society of America; the late Denise Levertov, also a Guggenheim Fellow and Shelley Memorial Award recipient and holder of the Robert Frost medal. If there is indeed a "feminist poetry movement" alive in the United States (as the title of one recent scholarly study claims) that has managed to win recognition from the poetry establishment, its acknowledged elders have over many years honored *Sojourner* by publishing in its pages and, now, allowing their work to be reprinted in this anthology.

More surprising, perhaps, is the list of respected experimental poets—a group probably not widely associated, in most readers' minds, with the feminist poetry movement—who have also found a place for their work in *Sojourner* and in this anthology. Leslie Scalapino and Lyn Hejinian, well-known poets based in the San Francisco Bay Area, have brought to *Sojourner* the kind of experimental writing (which fractures syntax as well as poetic forms of rhythm and rhyme and flouts boundaries between prose and poetry) that is associated with the L=A=N=G=U=A=G=E poetry movement as well as the L=A=N=G=U=A=G=E poets' interest in juxtaposing experimental poetry with reflective or theoretical prose about poetry. Thus their collaborative piece in this anthology, taken from their longer work *Sight,* is paired with both poets' meditations on what it was like to write collaboratively, to generate the compositional rules they observed in making the poem: a doubling of poetry with reflection on poetry that echoes the poem's thematic interest in pairing and what Hejinian calls "stereoptical seeing." Strikingly, this anthology's other long experimental piece, "Sappho's Gymnasium" by T Begley and Olga Broumas, is also a collaborative work. Where Hejinian and Scalapino order their experimental collaboration around doubled figures of sight, "Sappho's Gymnasium" is a poem (in its own words) of "marvelously saturated / physical gravity," of touch felt as holding and suspension. Yet readers who come to *Sight* after "Sappho's Gymnasium" in this anthology may well notice how Hejinian imbues even sight, potentially the most disembodied of senses, with muscular heft, imagining herself "walking off balance, hurrying forward / in order to compensate for the weight of my eyes and even then / leaning[.]"

Like *Sight* and "Sappho's Gymnasium," this anthology is a collaborative work, edited by Ruth Lepson with Lynne Yamaguchi, both of whom have served as poetry editors of *Sojourner*. In the larger sense, however, all anthologies are collaborations, not only between editors but among the various poets and poems anthologized. An anthology creates new contexts for poems, different from the context of their original publication; juxtaposed in this anthology, one poem leans into another, as Lyn Hejinian invites us to say, and talks to yet another. At the same time, though—as readers of *Sojourner* and its sister feminist publications will be well aware—anthologizing poems also and inevitably subtracts contexts from them.

To summon up those contexts for a moment: as I write this introduction, I have before me the poetry page of the October 2000 issue of *Sojourner*. Typically for *Sojourner*, the poems and their authors are diverse. April Dobbins's "For the Prisoners of Yazoo Federal Penitentiary in Mississippi" is her first published poem; Julie Grass from Los Angeles contributes "Mother Is a Mermaid"; Holly Pettit, who contributes "Silt," is not only a well-established figure in Boston poetry circles but also a former activist on behalf of Boston's homeless community. As is also typical for *Sojourner*, the poetry page echoes in intricate ways the feminist concerns of the newspaper as a whole. Readers of Pettit's "Silt," a meditation on the immigrant women—"Salvadorans, / Guatemalens"—who have crossed the "border's midnight riverbank," will also find in this number of *Sojourner* a review of Grace Chang's *Disposable Domestics: Immigrant Workers in the Global Economy,* featured in a regular column listing bestsellers from New Words, the Boston-area women's bookstore. April Dobbins's "For the Prisoners of Yazoo" keeps company in this issue with a feature article on women in prison and their struggles with the prison authorities' "deliberate indifference" to their physical and emotional health. A sidebar story alongside the feature article advises *Sojourner*'s readers of "What You Can Do" to help defend the rights of women prisoners; another column offers to connect readers with women prisoners seeking correspondents.

To compile an anthology out of poems originally published in *Sojourner* is inevitably to distance the poems from direct contact with this broad ongoing continuum of contemporary feminist culture. The poems anthologized become poetry with the implicit capital P: dateless and timeless as reprinted (except in instances where the author had originally chosen to incorporate a date into her poem) and surrounded by ample white space on acid-free paper rather than by *Sojourner*'s lively newsprint welter of journalism, argument, activism, and humor. By abstracting these poems from their original publication contexts in *Sojourner*'s feminist culture venue and presenting them together, grouped not by date or theme, say, but by the neutral alphabetical ordering of the authors' last names, the anthology form tacitly poses the difficult question: is there something in this collection that we might agree to call "feminist poetry," in which all of these poems could be said to participate, whose generic outlines the sum of these poems would limn? Perhaps so, even probably so, but in saying so we might bear in mind Lyn Hejinian's comments about her collaboration with Leslie Scalapino: "The 'we' of collaborations is not the we of a gang; instead it can be the we of supervention, the we of surprise." The same is true of the "we" of feminist poetry more generally.

《 《 《

For most readers of this anthology, perhaps the least surprising thing anyone could say about feminist poetry is that it proceeds from the assumption that the personal is political. As readers will be reminded, contemporary feminist poetry has created entirely new genres or subgenres of lyric poetry around the need to reinvent personal life as at once familiar and unwritten. Here is Ellen Bass, for example, writing in one of those genres, the midlife lesbian coming-out poem:

> This miracle of our passion is new
> a constellation not yet named.
> The love is old, familiar as your body stirring soup
> Lifting Sara to your lap, my pleasure in your gestures.
> I have waited this patient cycle of years to tell you.

Other poems in this anthology, by contrast, defamiliarize heterosexual relations. Sarah Fox and Naomi Feigelson Chase brood over women's alienation from their own desire. In "He Comes to Lie Down," Chase asks, "He comes to lie down in my bed and pretends I'm not here. / Or is he the absent one?" More brutally and graphically, in "Interruption" Fox pictures a coupling barely

this side of rape, the woman speaker's silence and bodily resistance commu-
nicating nothing to the man "knifing your stupid sex up and down my jeans":

> But you are only
>
> thinking YOU while I'm clenched
> against the wall, my hands
> behind my back. Remember this
>
> when you're again alone
> in your dark quiet room: I'm a shadow
> you can bend your body on
> but never through.

Exploring similar veins of alienated desire, Ruth Buchman's "Short Story"
recalls a first time going to bed with a man, while Elizabeth Rees's "Rockstar
Poet" imagines heterosex from the point of view of a male celebrity poet: "re-
gret chills his teeth" after his encounter with an adoring woman, and "tomor-
row / he will sing over her head." From a different perspective, however, Kate
Mullen's "Thin-legged Lover" addresses as "you" a woman (herself?) who
flaunts a distinct erotic preference for the cowboys of this world, with their
(for her) pleasurably stereotyped male bodies:

> You always did like your men well hung
> A thin-legged lover with arms outstretched
> With ribs you could knit your fingers through
> With a hollowed-out clavicle to dip your tongue in
> [. . .]
> A thin-legged lover you can mount anytime, anywhere
> And nail and nail and nail again.

Here is a version of female heterosexual desire as active, dominant, and even,
in a sense, objectifying. Without moralizing, Mullen asks us to imagine wom-
en as possibly having a stake in admitting the pleasures of such objectification,
perhaps in admitting something impersonal or alienated about desire itself,
that citadel of "the personal" in modern life.

Where there is the personal-impersonal politics of desire there will also be
the politics of personal relationships, and this anthology features a compel-
ling range of breakup poems, marriage poems, and divorce poems. Among my
favorites here is T Begley's and Olga Broumas's "Sappho's Gymnasium," a kind
of experimental, orgasmic lesbian epithalamion, or marriage song, that ends
in praise for

> my wife who is marvelously saturated
> physical gravity created by confession

when this was done an eggshell forms
us light hammering a spasm of sound[,]

which readers might set beside Gertrude Stein's "Lifting Belly" and other of
Stein's experimental poems memorializing her union with Alice B. Toklas. Less
ecstatically, Carol Baker's "Your Going" also imagines a relationship as a shell
or a vessel; but this one is empty, although not broken, a sacramental container
memorializing a relationship that both partners acknowledge to be in the slow
but inevitable process of ending:

How is it I am both bereft and content
and the dark so neutral it seems a blessing,
no impediment? A vessel scoured of anguish
where we lie not together, not apart
but both contained. In the great silver
bowl of night you will sleep when you arrive,
will curl south in the direction a compass
implies, toward me. And if your fingers graze
the bowl's unending rim they will touch mine.

"Let me not to the marriage of true minds admit impediment": Baker's echo
of Shakespeare's sonnet 116 ironizes and confers a certain grace on the way
these two lovers come apart.

The politics of the personal extend well beyond the romantic dyad, lesbian
or straight, in the poems of this anthology. Relations between mothers and
daughters loom large: Rebecca Baggett's "Barely Eight" muses on the impend-
ing puberty of her daughter Morgan, wondering how they will negotiate "that
neverland where young girls wander, / lost, for years, at war with mothers / and
themselves"; Linda McCarriston grieves at being severed by divorce from her
young son, torn out of her care and out of his own childhood by a judge who
deems it necessary that the boy be initiated into manliness by his father ("Kitch-
en Terrarium"). From the other side of the parent-child relationship, many
poets in this anthology record their efforts to care for ill and aging mothers and
grandmothers: Vanessa Haley writes in "Gangrene" of a diabetic mother, blind
for many years and now ready to be taken "ashore to the other side of blind-
ness"; Carol Potter's "White Hotel" tells of reluctantly placing her grandmother
in a nursing home. In "Old," Rosario Morales struggles with her own mortal-
ity in the image of her mother and grandmothers. Having anticipated aging as
the shedding of an inhibiting skeleton—"I knew thirty was what I was going
to be when I lost the skeleton I / wore, when I grew old, grew beautiful and
free"—she now finds herself crying "Stop! at ruckling ruches of skin / at soft
sags, / bags of tongue-tickling breast and belly." Similarly, in "The Raptor," her

mother's gradual death at home of lung cancer causes Molly Peacock to ponder her own: "Who knows what death I'll get exactly, / being daughterless, the line of begetting / neutralized, in hands beyond love."

More surprisingly, perhaps, this anthology features many eloquent and generous poems on the personal politics of fatherhood. Several poets contribute elegies for fathers and grandfathers. In "Fugue," Carol Dine discovers her love for, identification with, and independence from her father in the black pantsuit she buys for his funeral—"Like an usher, / or my father's son, the boy in the family he always wanted." Alma Stacey Allen's "Road Trip" remembers her father in connection with that great American mourning ritual, the automobile journey. Other poets find themselves linked to and separated from their fathers through identifications of class and ethnicity. Kathryn Kirkpatrick offers a painfully belated tribute to her working-class father whose failed effort to organize a special dinner celebrating his daughter's high school graduation symbolizes for her all the ways he "never believed in his own kindness" ("Class"). Speaking for many of the poets in this volume, Marilyn Zuckerman addresses her grandfather, who spent his every morning "thanking Jehovah" he was "not a woman," with the acknowledgment, "Still, old wanderer, / how I follow in your footsteps" ("In Every Pot and Closet").

Some of the ancestors summoned in the poems of this anthology are literary and cultural rather than familial. Among the most familiar genres of contemporary feminist poetry is the tribute poem to great women precursors, represented here by Rita Dove's "Sonnet in Primary Colors," celebrating the life and work of the painter Frida Kahlo. Cornelia Veenendaal, in "Sun-crossed," adds beautifully to the lengthening skein of women poets who have written on Emily Dickinson:

> In a straight chair
> at a small square table
> Emily Dickinson
> is writing
>
> *Make me a picture of the sun—*
> *So I can hang it in my room—*
>
> Her columnar self
> A gnomon in the light;
> now she crosses the seagrass mat
> barefoot to the Spice Isles.

Kate Rushin goes looking for W. E. B. Du Bois in the public library of Great Barrington, Massachusetts, modelling her quest after Alice Walker's search for her own ancestor in Zora Neale Hurston ("Looking for W.E.B."). Virginia

Woolf inspires Nadya Aisenberg's "The Woman in the Moon," with its glimpse of Clarissa Dalloway "shopping for green ribbon in The Strand," as well as Nancy Means Wright's "Acrophobia," in which a friend measures Virginia Woolf's famous prescription for women writers—five hundred pounds and a room of one's own—against the reality of a small Boston apartment where *To the Lighthouse* sits "next to the bottle of Zinfandel / and the mink oil bath beads by the four- / legged tub."

Beyond tribute to literary and cultural ancestors lie struggles with the older myths, struggles that generate another familiar genre of contemporary feminist poetry, the revisionist myth poem. In this anthology, Caroline Finkelstein's "Persephone's Notes," "Afterthought," and "Casus Belli" echo H.D.'s "Eurydice" and *Helen in Egypt* in their portraits of women harrowing the hells of literary tradition, women for whom men go to war, women exchanged as prizes of war and taught "to count / lice on the minotaur's back" ("Casus Belli"). Celia Gilbert asks "Questions about the Sphinx"; Jennifer Rose addresses a woman who committed suicide imagining herself as Alcestis waiting to be rescued by a Hercules ("The Suicide"). The politics of literary tradition are personal to the poets of this anthology.

Mediated as it may be by literary tradition, however, their relationship as feminist poets to poetic language is always intimately embodied. Thus Beckian Fritz Goldberg begins "Say" with an apostrophe to her own cold, stilled tongue—

Tongue, what are you doing up there in space
among the tunnels of birds and the about-to-snow,
still as the blush on far fruit?

I stand with only breath in my jaws, the absurd
fur on which I cannot place even a
finger.

—before turning to the lover beside whom her voice "fades like a scent." Language may fade, resist, still, or be opaque to these poets; but that is its value. As Eli Clare says in "Learning to Speak," comparing herself as a poet to a child to whom language comes with difficulty: "She had to learn / the muscle of her tongue." Readers of this anthology have before them twenty-five years of this learning to appreciate.

Poetry from *Sojourner*

Kathleen Aguero

Looking for Another Version

1.

We meet. We fall in love.
I spend evenings imagining
you leave me for another woman—
thin, beautiful.
I am noble. I wouldn't fuss.
Go. Leave me for some woman you can push around.
It's easier to begin with endings I control.

Never let the enemy know what's going on.
Never give that satisfaction.

2.

Is this what I mean when I say I'm independent—
I only know who I am by knowing I'm not you.
I'm not you or you
or you or you or you.

I daydream happiness—
blurred face smiling,
moony body without angles,
without motion.
It does not get anything done.

3.

"You are your own worst enemy,"
my mother said.

If I am my own worst enemy, do I go over to the enemy camp to
    make friends?
If friends become very good friends, they are no longer friends.
They are problems.
They will want something from you—
your time, your toothbrush,
your best stories to tell for their own.
You will not be left alone. You will not
be yourself. You will not get anything done.

4.

We agree to go our separate ways
and stay together.
I went my separate way—
yours, too.

To be all the tyrant that I can,
even looking for another version.

Working Mother

She has it down. Get dressed. Put the housecoat back on over the suit so
you won't have milk stains on the lapel, buttery fingermarks at the hem.
Once, inspired by an article in *Working Women's News,* she put the children
to bed in jogging suits so she didn't have to wrestle them into clothes the
next morning.

Drop them off with someone who will drop them off at school. Tag them
like suitcases so they won't get lost. Pump them with vitamins so they don't
get sick. Give them ice packs for fever so she can get in a morning's worth
of work before the day care teacher catches on.

She hears her daughter playing with dolls: "Hurry up. Get dressed. Do you
want me to be late again?"

She dreams of the toys and clothes strewn over the house accumulating un-
til one day as she leaves she can't shut the door no matter how she bangs
herself against it. Dust creeping out the window trails her to work. She feels
like a cartoon character: arms and legs stretched wide straining against two

walls that move relentlessly together until the figure between them is flat-tened like cardboard.

One day she carries the two-year-old under her arm instead of a briefcase, distributes diapers to the class while at home books are stacked in the sink waiting to be washed, essays tucked neatly in their beds.

Nadya Aisenberg

The Woman in the Moon

Maybe that day I met Clarissa Dalloway
shopping for green ribbon in The Strand
she was thinking of Jacob,
or the voyage to the lighthouse;

Drinking lemon tea and watching the moorhens
in St. James' Park, *I will give you my Apostle Spoons*,
she said, *or my olivewood beads.*
Do come and see me, it is so hot in town . . .

She walks in the moon garden at Sissinghurst
her swooping hat dappling in her face, the green ribbon
startling the white-petalled mind.

Alma Stacey Allen

Road Trip

Today I see what my father saw:
scenery that pains the eye with
contrast. A road like a cradle,
a green ache in the driven heart.

On the left a hawk snatches a snake
from his earthy pursuits, flies
high and waves him like a flag.
Real drama up there above the pavement.

A bus passes, windows full of ruined
faces that peer and smile behind
tinted glass. Shiny red bus with
billboard sides, Jersey plates in blue.

Orphaned late in life, I wish there
was somewhere I wanted to go, someone
I wanted to see. Instead, I taste old
teaspoons at the back of my mouth.

My life is moving too fast, time
compresses. I see the roadside
telephones and wonder what's the point
no one will answer, no one will come.

Carol Arber

Sketching in Barnstable

The space to the pad seems to be stocked
with those filmy, mobile particles or
are they reflections of things from the inside?

The light on the cape is no clearer than Cambridge,
I think; it's just that when the friend of the present weekend
abandons you because the anxiety gets to him,

there you are with nothing but fear climbing near your neck.
So you keep staring at the paper and the stuff between
you and the inviting white surface; it's nothing,

you might assure yourself, the space to the drawing pad.
It's nothing to put your mind on, nothing.
So you save yourself, keeping the hand
moving, a technical blue ship in this place

filled with bits of moving things, little hairs, filmy lights.

Rebecca Baggett

Barely Eight

for Morgan

Barely eight, already you are entering
that neverland where young girls wander,
lost, for years, at war with mothers
and themselves. "This can't be happening
yet," I protest to doctors, teachers,
mothers of your friends, who say it probably
is. Those goddamned growth hormones
they're feeding cattle, one suggests, more
cheerfully than not. They're all maturing
earlier—why, mine wears a bigger shoe than
I do, and she's only nine.

I'm not prepared for this. Your head has
topped my chin; you barricade yourself
inside your room, complain of us in your
diary, sob at imagined slights; and yet
you're reading Robin Hood and Oz and Narnia,
snickering when you see your parents kiss,
in love only with dogs and your own humor.
If I am caught unready, what of you, as you
ricochet between the little girl I have begun
to miss already, and the stranger I will someday
love, who stares at me now from my child's eyes,
plotting her ascension.

Carol Baker

Your Going

I have no doubt you will accomplish
this thing you are bent on, will proceed
in your one direction till the delicate
net that held us gives and you
tear free, gulping the great wind
of your separate life. Your going
is certain as your return, and the road
whose dark pines and firs you pass between
implies neither direction.

Even now your hands are on the wheel
and my heart spun out to its limit
hums and hovers more than a moment
over a state line before I reel it in.
Your going is a thing I read in these lines
written to forestall the knowing they reveal,
partaking in their intricate and clumsy
progress down the page of the present
movement which you are.

How is it I am both bereft and content
and the dark so neutral it seems a blessing,
no impediment? A vessel scoured of anguish
where we lie not together, not apart
but both contained. In the great silver
bowl of night you will sleep when you arrive,
will curl south in the direction a compass
implies, toward me. And if your fingers graze
the bowl's unending rim they will touch mine.

Jane Barnes

Passion at Forty

What will your landlady think of me
sitting on your porch for hours
waiting for you to come home?

Al, Look out there.
That girl's still on our stairs.
She's eating her supper now.
Out of a bag.
Camping out.
Do you think she'll sleep here?
A minute ago she wrote something
in a book. Can't she do all this
at her own house?

O, Wanda. Come and sit down.
Your program's just come on.

Now she's writing again.

Wanda. Stop it.

What will she think, dear?
Only that I'm crazy.
Never that I'm in love with you.

Ellen Bass

All the Trees

for Janet

February, 1982

I want to tell you
how can I tell you what I want to tell you:
the green of things that bloom in late February
the apple blossoms.
My daughter Sara tells me she went to an apple orchard:
"An orch-red," she explains, "is not just one tree.
It's all the trees." Janet,
when I say I love you
it's not just one tree.

What can two women mean to each other
unconnected by blood
or by the sweet release of sex?
"You don't come second with me," you say.
"The people I love, I love."

You ask for everything
and nothing—
no commitment
no weekly phone call or engagement.

Once you asked to sleep in my bed
the healing of heartbeat through the night,
but my husband was coming home late.
I held you, stroked

your forehead a moment longer
before separation.

I left my infant first with you.
When she wouldn't quiet
you suckled her from your small dry breast.
When I returned, she clung to your nipple.
"I hope you don't mind," you said.

I tell you I love you.
What I do not say is that we meet in my dreams—
our bodies.

April, 1983

The fragment ended there—*our bodies*
and the beginning of the next letter, a single
upstroke. I cannot tell
what word it was meant to begin.

Fear held my hand.
I carried the little notebook in my purse
a companion.

Eight years of friendship, a slow accumulation
like minerals suspended in water, settling
to rock, thin crust and another
the pressure of time and exposure, layer
upon layer.

I knew and I did not know.

February, 1977

Janet, I want to write for you of moons, and how the honey bees
thicken the flowering quince with their humming wings this day
of the new moon. How the robins with their dusky red breasts
and the jays and the sparrows feast on warm, heavy pyrecanthus
until they are drunk and fly in dizzy swirls. I would like to
write of the nights we live in each other's dreams, or how you
looked last night, your hair drawn back from your face, your
bones exposed, the green-blue iridescence of your blouse, the
way it changed color as you moved. I would like to make poems
of all these things, but they come to me only in glimpses these days.

April, 1983

Dreams. We met at night.
In sleep, my husband and your lover receded.
Your hesitation, my fears, meant nothing.
Luxuriant, like tropical growth
that green so intense it vibrates purple in the sun.
And thick, like my hair, tangled and wild between your fingers.

Mornings, I'd see you on the road.
I dreamt about you last night, you'd say.
I'd grin lightly, wanting to be in your dreams
unable to conceive another place to meet.

When you touched me, stroking my palms
massaging each joint of my fingers
kneading the flesh at the base of my thumb, I'd sigh;
the intelligence of your hands, how they
read the pathways of my muscles, nerves
mapping unspeakable desire.
Eventually, I dared to touch you back,
your hands, feet, shoulders, temples.
I couldn't think ahead.

The entire year before my divorce I was obsessed with you.
I'd picture the house rearranged. You
would have the large bedroom, wisteria by the window.
I, a bed in my study with a view of the oak.
I wanted you in my life, daily, moving through the kitchen
frying tortillas, settling out jalapenos, the bean pot simmering.
Nights you'd fall asleep listening while I read *Alice in Wonderland* to Sara.
Mornings, I'd hear the splash of water as you washed.
A simple harmony of days, contrast
to the violent friction of my married world.

When I finally left, I confessed I was in love with you.
Blunt, graceless, it was not an invitation, just a statement of fact.
"Do you know what you're saying?" you asked, stunned.
"Yes," I nodded.

Months passed. You were out of town.
I drove to you, radio singing me on.
I sped to love you, hoping you would take me.

After dinner and wine, talk and easy laughter
you brushed your teeth, I slipped on my nightgown.
There was detergent caked down the front.
"There's detergent caked down my nightgown," I said.
"A likely story," you said.
"No, really, do you have an extra?"
"No," you smiled.

I put on a t-shirt. You put on one too.
We slid into bed, you flicked off the light
and your shirt. "Oh," I said
"is that how we do it? in the dark?"

Your warmth. I sighed into the universe
your skin the fur of rose petals, sweet warmth
like roses in the sun.

When you kissed me, all the softness of summer brushed full against
    my lips
and my mouth opened like morning glories.
I was a child, sipping honeysuckle tips
lying by the full bush, sucking the juice, dizzy
with deep breaths of honey-laden air. Intoxicated
I was a bee entering the tulip cup, damp slope of green
large white feathers of geese in flight, feel the wind
fragrance swirling, yellow pollen shook loose like fairy dust
upon the veined transparent skin, sunlight
through thin ribbed petals.
Fluid with nectar, we hummed
with the contentment of bees and loved
our tongues, our throats.

I reached for the light. Your smile that night
was a treasure beyond surprise. I had thought about
kissing you, touching, being touched,
even your exquisite cry of wonder and the shudder of breath.
But I'd never imagined you would smile.

Your face shining up at me, the corners of your eyes fanned
radiating like a child's drawing of the sun.
This gift, brilliant and generous as stars.

Your face, your elegant bones, the slopes and planes, curve of jaw,
beauty I had known through my eyes now alive under my fingers.

I stroked the lines of your smile and remembered being twenty
in love with a boy whose hair was soft as yours against my cheek
caressing his laugh lines with one fingertip. Something
about your smile, smell, warmth, this utter pleasure
that's lain quiet since then. Through all the other passions and
    commitments
no one until you. You reached inside me
your hand rain dancing
and I, the swollen clouds, poured.

Janet, we fly together. We swim through air
pushing up weight with great strokes, scooping.
We sail out over ocean at night, shoreline behind
the stars glisten, the damp black sky glistens
and we rise, gliding cool and silent in the dazzle.

This miracle of our passion is new
a constellation not yet named.
The love is old, familiar as your body stirring soup
lifting Sara to your lap, my pleasure in your gestures.
I have waited this patient cycle of years to tell you.

Now I swell like September apples, I am ripe
with offering. Janet, when I say I love you,
I don't mean just one tree. I mean
all the trees, the orchard, the grove
and the whole wild woods beyond.

Robin Becker

Incarnate

I spot him at the water's edge with his daughter,
a revised child from his new, corrected family. Waves
roll in and cover my father's feet, waves tumble the
heavy brown shoes of brokerage, precarious place settings,
camp trunks stuffed with our old clothes. In his mind,
my father places each one of us on a separate beach, like
a shaman scattering the poisons.

He grasps the child's hand. He has become the family
man my mother always wanted, dreaming up improvements
he will make around the house. When he sees me, he asks
forgiveness in a voice he has discovered since he was my
father. "Sure," I say. "Sure, dad." I can see that he is
happy and I weep; when he was ours, he hated beaches, he
hated being seen. Now he walks like an Old Testament king,
splendid David or great King Saul, wise with pain.

The Subject of Our Lives

The storm has started and they say it won't stop.
Not for you, hanging on in the office after everyone has left.
Not for the ponies in my friend's paddock, huddled and still
and turning white. I know from your voice that you like
this moment—a Friday afternoon, the city between us, a few hours
of paperwork before you can think of dinner or a movie

or sex. I have been thinking about the snowstorm, and about a woman
in Chicago who put me on skis and ordered me to follow her
into the woods. That was years ago, and I've stopped thinking
about her, except during blizzards, everybody powerless and stuck
without milk or cream. Now I see that love is really
the subject of our lives: the authority with which you opened

your jacket and placed my hand, rigid, near frostbite,
against your breast, waiting for the heat to make its miraculous
leap; the gentle rabbi leading my parents from my sister's grave.
The ponies stir at the sound of grain hitting a metal bucket,
carried by a woman who regulates their hungers. How many times
have I confused hunger and love, love and power? My head ached

for years, it seemed, following someone's beautiful back.
My sister wouldn't sleep or wake beside one person long enough to
learn something. *Trust me,* you say, and I'm struck by the force of
your voice, the imperative form of any verb spoken in bed. Come home.
No, stay where you are. Longing will serve us while snow thickens
the sidewalks, delays the subways, tightens every street in town.

Selective Memory

Light fills the great spaces
behind government buildings in Washington, D.C.

I'm in love, standing outside the National Gallery
and I'm in love again in Dupont Circle.

How delicately two people re-acquaint themselves with passion,
each coming from her separate life, focused as a narrow canyon

or a dim street in New York, walking that boulevard
of engagements that is daily life. What I have never managed well

is part of me forever, a friend lost to suicide
or the sadness of family life. And now my body wants to live

alongside yours, as you stood in the hospital room with me
where I had come to hold my grandmother's hand. You were right;

we have to let go of the future the way I let her go back
to her bed. Days later, in the Blackwater Reservation, snow lit

the trails we skied. The argument we were having
comes back to me like the habit of fear. When I tell the story

of how we met, my memory is selective, looking for the words
to the best story, though the one that is true is more difficult

to tell, because it leaves everything open.

T Begley and Olga Broumas

Sappho's Gymnasium

from Prayerfields

for healthy cells please remember
if touching something i am touched
hand foot and head
and then the tablet is broken
off everything
is beautiful acting out
—

nothing more is desired
nothing more is wanting
our sorrow a holiness so set about
so pressed upon we taste and see
the small salt here is
this tender helpless human life
that steep withdrawal we
knew this creek a mile away
—

sunspun into this work and need
to come devotedly without
shame upon yourself by this least
sweeping it is making
white on their deeply bent backs
and a ribbon in her hair please
white and standing out and so soft
and translucent through which
your body was visible
sunlit the mall of your back

—

there is no other blankness like you
I can rarely tell where your eyes
are focused into the plexus
of the lens and the way
your mouth and throat worked
in forgetfulness
if this one holds me so
pleasurable does so long
enough I came visibly to
love

—

the lamp stands on the little table
and the little table is spread the bed
is a prayer and here is this room in a near
dead darkness in which I first
know you undo the garden of exceeding
happiness after each flush I
end up crying
after the ships
called bluets and innocents

—

one's mother body slightest
accidental brushing her own hand
full of impalpable restraints swaddling
cradleboard there is nothing
to prevent a father from
bathing his infant then there are
those who can love the
neonate and just-walking

—

only the analyst of souls knows how
to exhume them to the breathing it is necessary
for the caller to anoint
the newborn

—

becoming the wife of my beloved she was
carried to my father the impossible world is
all around us indistinguishably
one is this act the cause can be
anywhere

—

the road did not continue beyond the spot where
he had stopped and the unforgiven
contracts touch and
be done if I can rest now if I can rest
in the singularity of
your body the way
you sleep in my open palm

—

you
whose back is soft whose meaning is
soft proprioceptive
touch netting and releasing the thin tears
she always drank from her own
glass

—

grief that is not expressed I have saved
and at times recovering my natural
voice I sit by the death bed she is
so beautiful a transparence one speaks
is the beginning of
memory of sensation let me make
it good light being unborn

—

let us begin with pleasure
from there derive meaning or discover
I put my hammock next to yours
I committed all the necessary murders within
myself
to acquire faith
an infinitesimal hope came along
only then shall I prepare what I would
prepare for myself

—

alone daily peace
to honor without coveting
the possibility of life
without meeting boundaries or ever turning back

—

with my wife who is marvelously saturated
physical gravity created by confession
when this was done an eggshell forms
us light hammering a spasm of sound

Sally Bellerose

Bye Bye Barbara

She went slowly,
with very little meat
between the skin and spine.

Still, until the end she tried
to make a straight line of bone.

Hungry all the time.

The big surprise was her eyes,
how they bulged with the world
getting bigger in her orbits
as she died.

Deborah Boe

Jigsaw Puzzle

An entire day spent scrutinizing
these pieces of a Paris boulevard.
First—all pieces with a straight edge
fitted together on the borders. Then
clumps of pieces of identical color
or pattern. Looking at the picture
on the box is cheating, but I always
look. Then I know, for instance,
which border is up, which down.
Pieces of clouds look unlike themselves,
some white, some gray, but they belong
together. Pieces of a wrought-iron fence,
vertical black after vertical black.
There are parts meant to fool me,
cuts so similar I try and try
to link them. But the hem of a lady's dress
does not belong to the clouds. No matter
how long I insist. Sooner or later I need
an intermission. I walk outside.
I lie on the lawn with the sun.
Some things belong together. Some don't.
I wonder. Will I ever learn this?

Marguerite Guzman Bouvard

Landscape

The dimensions are dizzying; peaks
unraveling the sky, light sheer

as rock unbroken by leaves or shrubs
or the humble shadows of passersby.

In this wilderness, I must invent
my own markers, a way of describing

distances only my body knows.
I'm like the first settlers who tried to stake out

a plot in rampant space: nights,
the frail structure of belief crumbles.

And yet you look at me and see a woman
like any other; you don't see

the landscape of illness, the cliffs
within myself I scale each day.

Polly Brown

This Is for Megan

my tamed predator, so old now
the wayward chickens from
next door walk under her nose
and she sometimes refuses
the chase, which she once felt
as an obligation to honor,
to doghood. This is for Meg

who speaks to me in the inflections
of her eyebrows, her sighs,
her shivering fits, her prancing;
her attraction to bad smells:
manure, dead fish, dead skunks, dead
anything, rotten anything—disguises,
all disguises;

and this is for Megan in her long-suffering
stubbornness, her refusal to hush
when hushed, to get out
of a place where she's hidden and hard
to reach, under the bed, under the bushes,
under the porch, in her deafness,
in her aging—that trap we all hurry

to enter and then find we cannot leave—
like a cat up a tree, like a woman in a
tight marriage, like a country about
to declare war, like a child waiting birth,
she is wedged deeper and deeper in her lame
old self, she yelps louder and louder
to be let in, to be let out

Ruth Buchman

Short Story

It begins in a small room.
The party dress her mother bought her, her carefully
combed hair, his dumb hands.

Unclothed, the sudden distance of their bodies.
She could close her eyes, see him again
in those pants, the stiff new shirt,
how his lips looked wet before he kissed her.

At least he is not heavy.

Later, they can't forget that strange
pushing between them. How, when their bodies joined, each
was alone in surprise, unaware of the other.

If they could sleep, there would be waking, the touch
of a glance between them. But she wants a shower,
and he wishes he'd learned to smoke, wishes he'd learned
a thousand things to make it up to her, and to himself.

It will be years before he discovers
a sweet memory of her body
clothed in the sheets, one arm over the covers,
waiting. She'll remember his odd laugh, the way
he covered himself with his hands, ashamed.

Claudia Buckholts

Old Woman Reclining

I lie in bed smelling the scent of cork
from the panels that line the walls,
looking at the list of what remains to do.
I think how my nephew has named his second daughter
Persephone, though her eyes are blue as cornflowers,
and she plays in the sand by the back window
all day, singing her one song: *ga, ga, ga*
and propped by pillows, in my room
I hear her, and smile.

My children gather to be of help,
and I drink the tea they bring,
look among their lucid eyes
and say, *I have forgotten so much.*
But nevertheless, I remember.
There is that child singing in the garden
to remind me that under the daystar
I live, and this is the cramped house
of my body, that now I am leaving.

Now in my thoughts I am out there with her,
sunning myself, watching the wind ruffle the grass
like the fur of a giant animal.
I fold my hands, the hands of an old woman,
together in my lap, and think, *this
is the body of earth that I have loved.*
From amid the myriad distances that open
among the stars, I hear the child singing
the small song of her life.

Leslie Burgess

The Prostitute's Notebook

Learning the Language

Like the turning of things
I pass into the language
of this place as if led
here, my lips rounder,
a darker red, my voice
the full range of water.
I drip words as if I'm
the source of a hot spring
staining the rock
with my constant murmur.
I say *french or fuck*
becoming steam
over a trapped pool.

Or, I'm the glazed
lake of the desert
shimmering words
to you, *come here,*
come, until you fall
into me hearing
my harsh sandy laugh
trick, trick.

You see, it's all a matter
of timbre. These words
can roar like a river

crashing through its dug
bed screaming *mother
fucker,* spreading you
flat. Or, they can
stretch out prone
as an iced-over lake
giving you your face back
perfect as it seems.

Black Carol, Singing

Ya'll called her
that funky black bitch.
I said it too.
Loud, slamming
my glass of VO & water
hard on the bar. I
called her crazy.
The night they took
her away we watched
from the window.
Carol, jumping from car
to car. From the hood
of a Chevy to some pimp's
lime green Lincoln. That
mothafucka gonna be one
mad nigga, we said.
Carol kept singing
somebody tole me
to de-liv-a this message,
her voice an arrow,
her smile a din in her face
that stayed up when she
was down. I watched her
bouncing leaving her smile
in the air like prisms
flash light on a wall.
She ripped her white blouse off

her black breasts dancing out
in the night and I remembered
her another night unbuttoning
it slow for the rich trick,
her smile toward me
as I did the same.

Carli Carrara

On Weekends

On weekends, my husband pays the bills, files away our life
    in folders, neatly labeled, paints a doorjamb blue.
Sometimes he takes me out for pizza and, after, to the matinee,
    where we always sit in the fourth row from the back.
Every night he hunkers down in front of TV, devoted
    to game show glitter, reruns of "Victory at Sea."
At first, I'd stay, the way I stayed with our daughter
    until she drifted off to sleep,
but then I moved into the next room, reading in the winged-back chair,
    the door between us closed.
Now and then, I go out at night, alone, or with friends to classes,
    weekend workshops on "Women, Passion, and Change,"
trying to unlearn the disciplines I allowed or inflicted
    upon myself to still the longing.

Did it happen in the night as I dreamed or in the shower while I
    conditioned my hair?
I keep thinking of Lot's wife, who moved too soon; I'm afraid
    I'm moving too slowly and tell myself
a thing cannot freeze if it is moving. Should I rush out now, with
    just a set of clean clothes, scattering family photos
down the driveway, or pack with care the lamp my grandma gave me,
    satin glass, the color of fresh blood,
its wick raised and freshly clipped? Was it all the dishes
    I stacked, all the leftovers I scraped down the drain?

Do I take the dog?

Naomi Feigelson Chase

He Comes to Lie Down

He comes to lie down in my bed and pretends I'm not here.
Or is he the absent one? In the castle, a million
tiny wires fire the grand chandelier.

He comes to lie down in my bed as the moon climbs
the night fence and takes a hundred sharp thoughts
with it. The grass is bright with splinters,

glass sharp as spikes
Baba Yaga sets before her house,
impaled with her false lovers' heads.

There's always a straw bed for love,
a cold afternoon,
followed by real morning.

There's always water freezing
in rusted pipes, in ponds, in tidal pools.
A drop is the beginning of an ocean.

There's always pleated matter in the universe,
there's always God's Bishop carrying Christ into some holy war,
a president refusing to govern or pay his taxes,

a doctor in a clean white coat, experimenting on Jews, Blacks,
homosexuals, etcetera. Or soldiers wiring triple A batteries
to blast a traitor's testicles.

He comes to lie down in my bed fully clothed
in his dog face, his navy whites, his army fatigues,
his wolf habits. I'd give my life
to teach him to refuse his.

Plenty

At summer's end, I come home to wilderness
in my garden, tomato stalks dragging,
fruit rotting on the ground, escaped
marbles hidden under furry
leaves wilting like bad ideas.
Only the eggplant behaves; pale green sentinels,
agreeably uprights, "Long Toms" thin and glossy,
"Black Magics," big bottomed, shining, ready. . . .

Linda allowed this to happen, remembering *mabiki,*
or "thinning out," a Japanese farm-word
for "infanticide." Instead of weeding, she hides
pictures of her parents in the garden—as her mother did—
because they love flowers, sets before their photos
the day's first bowl of rice. I think of jade dishes
in an emperor's tomb, bow to her ancestors
as I harvest, crawling around the raveled stalks.

The garden insists on growing,
doesn't need order. I'm the needy one,
craving the rank tomato smell,
the thorny touch of the cuke
more than the scent of a man's body.
They stay the summer, each hot day,
the fruit riper. I take them at their best,
to savor all winter.

Next summer I will fill the garden with pictures,
my children looking up at sunflowers,
my parents gazing evenly at strawberries.
I will set out small pots of soup, spoons.
People will grow there, statues of Venus sprouting arms,
twig dolls dancing among the corn.
I will move from the house, feet rooting
in corn, hair turning to silk,
giving birth to my children,
my bed in rosemary.

My Mother, Listening to Flowers

"Loud," she whispers, "common, like me,"
red fingernails pulling leaves
from her flowered housedress, pointing
to marigolds she planted by the garage door.
"At night, I hear them screaming."
I ask her, "What do they say?" "Scream,"
she corrects, "plague, I will drown
fleeing Egypt. Ten years of bad luck."

In the nursing home, she speaks maybe
a word a year. Can't or won't,
we don't know. When the nuns walk her
between them, in the garden,
"More water," she says.

Eli Clare

Learning to Speak

Three years old, she didn't talk,
created her own sign language,
didn't walk but stumped
all over the house on her knees
growing thick calluses. I am
her inheritor: words slow dance
off my tongue, never leap
full of grace. They hear
blank faces, loud simple replies.
She practiced the sounds *th, sh, sl*
for years, a pianist playing endless
hours of scales. She had to learn
the muscle of her tongue.

This Familiarity

Each time I come back
the quiet startles me like
a bobcat, the attempt
to memorize fails and
I walk the same
bend in the river
from swimming hole to

maple tree hanging out
over the water, roots half-naked,
this time will I find it
uprooted, ready to be washed away
by the next long rain?

Later hiking the stream uphill
to the shale slide, looking for
recent blowdowns, tangle
of alder and tan oak, sometimes
myrtle, next year's firewood.

Christmas Eve hunting agates
barefoot on Battle Rock Beach,
what can I do with this familiarity
like the color of river
after the first storm?

Lynne Cohen

Body Doubled

Inside every thin woman is a fat one,
struggling to get out.

My other self is floating above a crowd
of admirers. She is huge and weightless
and filled with blackforest cake and mousse
pie and salty potato chips with ridges and black-
tipped pretzels and real ice cream with whipped
cream and hot bittersweet fudge. When she lands,
she bounces ever so slightly and steadies her
abundant self with two liters of classic coke.
Nobody can put his arms around her, but everybody
wants to. When the music begins, she dances with
abandon. She is dressed in a wild tropical caftan,
like a member of some amazonian sorority.
The band pauses for her refreshment and she grate-
fully acknowledges the nachos with cheese and
jalapeños. She orders out for little white boxes
of sweet and sour and fried rice and cookies that
tell her what to do next. She writes a book about
how to communicate with everywoman's enemy, food.
She is invited to appear on a talk show
by a popular host who once pushed a wheelbarrow
filled with seventy-two pounds of fat on stage,
just to show the world how she was weighed down.
Now she is saved and can eat french fries in public.
The new Saviour does a church tour, eats all the hosts

and doesn't care. Her body doubled is sexless
and desirable. She cuts her hair short to accentuate
the moon that is her face in folds. She is the new
Christ, embodied in something more than human.
Men love her. Women want to be her.
She says, "food is love."
She travels the world to eat with all her disciples.
She visits a tribe of friendly cannibals and learns
to really love her fellow man.

To prove her universal love, she sits down to each supper
as if it were her last.

Martha Collins

Re:composition

It's easy to throw away if you've always
had it. Easy to do in if it's
a girl, especially Dad's.

But if you got weaned from the mother
tongue before you learned to speak
for yourself, if you throw

like a girl anyway and it lands back
in your lap—it might be something.
Just something. You could use.

Elizabeth Crowell

Portraits of the Ladies

In Monet's landscape, this woman fades away,
she is so barely marked in place.
She strolls through poppy fields, her sway
is flushed into the sun. She had no face.

Degas' dancer marks her toes in place;
her costume clouds the mirrored walls.
We only see the luscious flush without a face
as she moves from what the mirror caught.

And at *Folies-Bergère,* the cloudy, mirror wall
does not reflect the woman as she stands.
She has been moved away from what she saw
to face only the mirror of a man.

Renoir reflects on a woman as she dances
in a skirt-filled elegy of light.
Lautrec mirrors her facing men for chances
taken in some starry, starry night.

Gauguin paints elegies to city lights
on long, green islands where she is drawn
to the moon and violet lust of starless nights,
the spirit bodied, naked as bone.

And on Long Island, William Chase draws
her dangling in a white-dressed motion,
distant on beaches colored bone
against the intense blue of summer ocean.

John Dewing shows only the white dress, leaves motion
to the grip of mirrors, chairs and walls,
as a woman keeps a toneless devotion,
postured in greyish, painted squalls.

The lines of chairs and light, the depth of walls
collapse her breasts and arms and legs and face.
Jaded and bare in *Les Demoiselles d'Avignon*
she is the body where the landscape fades.

Cortney Davis

What Man Might Kill

On November 29, 1988, Susan Galvin and
Martha Alsup were brutally murdered on a
remote beach on the island of Anguilla. Does it
matter to us exactly why Susan and Martha were
murdered? Isn't it enough to know that they were
two women traveling alone . . . ?
—*Sojourner,* January 1989

1

He lights a cigarette
begged from the sheriff who kept them

from lynching him, *hanging your crazy ass,
you understand?* He nods, and his fear

is a pocketful of stones.
When he was a boy he took his father's canoe,

dragged it over coarse shells to the beach
where sand turned smooth as skin. He slid his legs

into the wooden hatch and paddled out,
like a small man wedged inside another man.

He became a dot bobbing on the horizon
under a seabird's distant ellipse,

he paddled until he thought he'd drown.
Then he turned to see his island

indifferent as a woman sleeping,
her arms up over her head

toward Captain's Point, sun blinding him
as if she'd forgotten a mirror by her side.

2

On Sundays the voices of women
circle him like seabirds
and the sea in the curved harbor
hisses and tumbles back, not like
children playing but like firesmoke rolling.
His eyes are black as the grackles
that peck nits from goats grazing aimless
by the churches. And no half-moon shows

below his iris. His mother was glad.
She believed that white silver,
like a pared fingernail,
meant death. He sang in the choir,
in the blue peeling churches,
but he felt death in the quiet sheath of water
that sealed over his body, in the way
the salt dried and pinched his skin.

3

Finally, it was the women on the beach.
He watched them through vines of seagrape
as he plucked the ripe berries.
He saw how they considered each other,
how they drew one-finger paths
through sand crusting the other's skin.
They were overcome with a rapture

he'd seen women give into at church:
The presence of something holy
on the salt-skim of their lips,
how one woman spoke the prayer of another
with the curve of her tongue. The sun rose
in bright lines over the ends of the world.
He went crazed, the cops said later.

4

Through the window slit of his cell
the low scrub of island disappears at nightfall
and the sea pinpoints beneath the moon
like confetti scattering.

Under the tide the sand is stone
and shell crushed a million years;
anything living relentlessly knit
into the firm white matrix of silica

and otolith. His cigarette ash falls.
There is a sound in the dark, the entrance
of a cormorant into water, the bucket-mouth
scooping a fish that couldn't turn away,

just risen from beneath the breakers,
having seen the moon.

Carol Dine

Excerpts from "Fugue"

in memory of my father

IV

I take Douglas to visit his grandfather. He's 13 and he
doesn't want to go. He looks at my father's face, and his eyes
move fast to the TV as if they were burning. They chat,
and I hear the words "baseball" and "homework." I'm eavesdropping,
hear my father say he has a present for Douglas. He reaches
beside his bed. "It's my Harvard ring," he says.
"Try it on your middle finger."
"Maybe I'll go to Harvard someday," Douglas says as he
slides the gold ring halfway down his finger. I can tell he's
trying not to cry.
Last week my father gave my brother-in-law his golf clubs.
He also gave my uncle some of his sweaters,
and an old friend his winter coat with the fur collar.
I want something, anything. But I can't ask.
He doesn't give things to girls.

V

I can't stall any longer. I have to buy an outfit for
my father's funeral. I go to a discount store and browse,
try on a few dresses that make me look too tall.
I'm about to leave when a fat salesgirl runs after me.
"Did'ya see this?" I stare. It's a black linen pantsuit,
perfectly plain, perfectly tailored. "It's a designer,"
she says. "$90—a steal." I try it on, standing very

straight, almost holding my breath. Like an usher,
or my father's son, the boy in the family he always wanted;
he was going to name me Warren.
"Can I wear this to a funeral?" I ask the salesgirl.
"Whose?"

Rita Dove

Sonnet in Primary Colors

This is for the woman with one black wing
swept over her eyes: lovely Frida, erect
among parrots, in the stern petticoats of the peasant,
who painted herself a present—
wildflowers entwining the plaster corset
her spine resides in, that flaming pillar—
this priestess in the romance of mirrors.

Each night she lay down in pain and rose
to the celluloid butterflies of her Beloved Dead,
Lenin and Marx and Stalin arrayed at the footstead.
And rose to her easel, the hundred dogs panting
like children along the graveled walks of the garden,
until Diego appeared as a skull in the circular window
of the thumbprint searing her immutable brow.

Frances Driscoll

Real Life

But in real life, I begin. But Doug
interrupts: What happened that night was
real life. I don't know what he is
talking about. Real life is my sister
studying the bankruptcy notices each week
in the paper and continuing to have
difficulty with her soft consonants.
My psychic finding in the cards arrows
of love, waters of life. My son saying
I am the most dimwitted person he knows
and bringing home from a concert a pair
of bottled blondes from Mississippi,
escapees from a senior trip, who refuse
to respond to my questions—Where
is the rest of the class. Where are
your chaperones. Rinsing dishes
in the bathroom sink after the kitchen
faucet explodes without warning and, tired
of Electra shedding on the blue Chinese
plates, working to clear in the cabinet
space some builder allotted without
me in mind a shelf she can call her own.
Real life is Diana writing from Head
of the Tide, Maine, she is having a good
time fixing broken furniture and lamps.
Mary Kay eating potato chips with raisins
still so mad with the father of her children

for coming down with pneumonia after that
camping trip when she was the one who
deserved it. Bonnie, after reconciling
with a man denied tenure, making humming
sounds swallowing lettuce spread with jam.
In real life, a girlchild swings from the
flowering tree branching out over my terrace.
You know the secret of trees, she calls down
to her friend. You want one, you
find one. In real life, my chest tightens
and I forgive all the white blossoms
her careless legs have sent to the ground.
Not this girl. Never this girl. Not
in real life.

Nancy Esposito

Doing Good

All morning I've passed from window to window, shadowing
sunlight on my cat, preferring, rather, to cast shadows
like a snow sky on the lot below me next door. When
was it I began to despise people of conviction, if not
last night after the storm or this morning in full
cold light, watching the Boy Scout leader
and his grown son yank a sapling pine out of
the ice. Now the chain saw eating at a plank
of pine, at this height like amplified guitar
playing in my inner ear. By the end of tomorrow, the jerry-
built rectangle will seem a *sui generis* miracle, the patches
here and there of miserable earth overcome. I remind
myself, after two hours of a movie shot
in an abattoir, that every species eats on another
species. That it is proprietary pride
in this crowded cityscape where we live
against one another, cinder block by aluminum
siding, our cars and pickups huddled
on the streets and in the drives like a circle
of covered wagons or bunkers dug out of ice.
All morning I've avoided the north windows, the blur
of red, white, and blue in a strong wind, like ribbon
candy, waving to what's right. And I, above it all
smug in my categories and indifferent
to any chance to be wrong.

Liz Fenton

Places

I have been looking all over for a place to start from,
and there are many, but none of them quite places
to be. Rather each is a place of vantage
from which one can see, or barely see,

other places, most apparently reasonable habitations
from which to proceed, but impossible to get to.

In Kurdistan the babies fall off their families
like small brown acorns, one in every tent
shrivelling and leaking and lying still.
In Bangladesh they just float away on the water.

Most likely everyone's in a place, and everyone's
in a vantage, and we spend too much time craning our necks
trying to see or imagine how the other place is.

In what I would call a real place, the sound of footfalls
is of the same volume as voices, and both voice and thud
are unmistakably familiar. That is, they arouse
no fear, and can only be heard by strangers.
The people in the places don't hear them

separately from the cream-colored wallpaper
or the bang of wood chimes superimposed on crickets.
This is a way of saying that a place has dinnertime
and then it has evening—with enough personal commitments

one to the other, and all past discussion,
to put together a genuine evening
of interlacing dusk and maroon, until it too decomposes
into much later, too late to sit out in the cool anymore.

It may be evening where I am, certainly,
but since this isn't a real place I should sooner imagine
evenings in places such as I describe,

where someone else's cough can be heard in the belly
and it's so warm that you turn, and giggle
and juggle an ice cube in your hand.

Caroline Finkelstein

Persephone's Notes

There is a shapeliness in grief

and in silence, in the snow, a remembered thunder
like a bee, like a ribbon in the youngest child's hair,

a booming and a recalled view
we call a meadow, flowers in the meadow.

So the world is full of formal nattering and rules,
music and the rule of random, consequence

and precincts.
Below this world is hell.

        ☾ ☾ ☾

In hell I learned the uses for the body.
Underneath: like this.

And I am in it voiceless.
Then the greyness, the hell of huge indifference.

        ☾ ☾ ☾

That there never is a moral.
That black birds gather in wet meadows

early in the spring and peal
like metal and with cherries on their wings.

I want to because I do, he said, *beautiful, I want to.*

Afterthought

Had I died—but I did not

die, no, even in the shade I was
warm, a body with all its fingers.

That body still exists, permitted

to remember versions
of a woman and a boy, each

nearing one another, vying
in the semi-darkness

for power wholly
absolute. Think how

their reaching for sensation
is familiar in the raw world

where anodynes for cruelty are
cruelty. I remember

almost everything I've done since that initiation,
everything fierce and inconsistent

that reflects on nothing in particular

except the nature of humanity: anguish
in a few words of poetry—

so the daffodil emerges from its raked, naked bed,

white petals, white eye open.

Casus Belli

Miss third-person-singular-about-to-be-devoured, she's
the girl walking into randomness, the girl watching the girl

walking into randomness, walking into dangers.
They're giving her shoes because she's the girl

walking toward a swaying; they're giving her dark eyes,
giving her light hair, a blouse with buttons, jeans and a flower

(they always give a flower). They're giving her a landscape of
field and sidewalk, exurb and mall, and bushes

burning in the summer; they're teaching her to count
lice on the minotaur's back, and screams

of birds in the air—
She's walking in the wind and she has a coat;

they've given that to her; they say:
a nice navy wool coat, look how pretty

she is in it, what a cut,
how very shapely, how unusual—

They want to say *unusual* and say it really often;
they practice at the vanity; in the bathroom steam

they slowly form the words: *how un-u-zhu-al.*
They form the vowels behind their teeth.

She's watching smoke do tricks in the steam; it's
the breath of a trembling bull like spume off the water in fog;

she's watching; she's swaying; they say
they have pills for the swaying. For walking

they've given her shoes, unusual shoes,
unusual girl, Miss Archetype-neophyte-lady-of

sorrow, neophyte queen of the spring, unusual mouth
their hands clamp down on, their very justified hands—

Janice Finney

Lightning and Thunder

      I unplug
the TV, the endless
banter, and we sit
in the dark. Cramping,
cradling my belly, I lie
back on the couch.

   Thunder cracks,
rattles the stainless
silverware, salad tongs
nailed over the stove.
Outside fire sirens
whine like big babies
that won't quit. You smoke
a low tar, speak
of white cranes in Wisconsin.
They're purity in its purest
form. Nothing touches them
except the rain.

         I wish
I were in Wisconsin within
ear-shot of the cranes.
I could gather up the pure
wherewithal to tell you
of today today and not wait for time
to cloud things over
like a chain smoker
by the minute. I'd cry

a little and tell you
as little as necessary
without saying word for word
I got rid of the cry-baby baby
we made but already I can hear
you hearing of it.

Sarah Fox

Interruption

When a man is ashamed to masturbate,
and instead waylays a woman . . . he
regards her as a kind of human spittoon.
—Germaine Greer

You glutton up my stairs,
stung with wine and spangled and
demand hot tea, candles.

I had been reading
my dictionary before you cracked my bed-
room open with your ardent

buzzing. Now you quake shut my book and swag-
ger
over to perform your odd
gymnastics on my face; the teeth

of your whiskers claw my breath
away. If I weren't so
impatient I'd ask

you immediately
to leave. But all that
explaining doesn't attract an ear

when you're knifing your stupid
sex up and down my jeans, my
navel. As if this box

of a mouth and these stone
knuckles wouldn't give you a clue.
But you are only

thinking YOU while I'm clenched
against the wall, my hands
behind my back. Remember this

when you're again alone
in your quiet dark room: I'm a shadow
you can bend your body on
but never through.

Kathleen Fraser

One is whole. One is not

for Joanne Brackeen, jazz pianist

Never does it
come from cold number. White
throws away black, the keys
are put there swiftly.
Intentional lights filter straight
to where the baby is yet breathing music,
but not in this world. Yet swimming,
yet in the small
of her back, are not threes and
fours there?
Five attaches itself to hands and feet.
Top most mast of each hand afloat,
waving or reaching, not knowing
when the air hits some music. Some heart
thudding louder
or softer, wherever ear lands: Up
or down. Smelling out numbers.
Saying song is one,
instead of singing it. The heart's little
edges, ragged patch, dry and distinctly wet.
Water and distillation. Hesitation.
One is whole. One is not enough. One
leaves out two.

Erica Funkhouser

Lilies

Not days, not years,
these flowers mark
a less certain span.
The bulbs start up
months before opening;
by July they're heavy
with buds and tall enough
to shade me as I stake
the spikes too weak to carry
their own abundance.

They smell of clove
and yesterday's funeral
for a friend whose rare bloom
overtook her whole life.
I lift the white trumpets
and trace velvet streamers
back to the dark throat
of the trumpeteer.
From the churchyard
we watched the sky fade
beneath the weight of noon.
The windmill on the island
never moved.
Fanning the heat from our faces,
we embraced briefly
as the bells emptied
their black pollen
into the sea.

Kinereth Gensler

Bowl with Pine Cones

I fill my pockets with pine cones and empty them
in this bowl. Wherever I've been, I empty them.
The cones look alike.
Densely packed or open, small, large,
white pine or ponderosa, they look
more like each other than anything else—
the fruit, its seed long gone, of the evergreens.

In the Maine woods, I rock in a hammock
slung between pine trees. My parents
lean against a birchbark fence, watching.
They are very young.
They wear knickers and brown sweaters.
They look many-layered, lapped and overlapping.
I can tell they'll become
dry brown fruit, that they'll last.

Dust gathers on the pine cones.
They last and last.

Celia Gilbert

Questions about the Sphinx

I wonder who she was and how she got there
with her improbable get-up
of wings and those heavy lion haunches,

some sort of act, something to wow
them in the provinces where she was
stuck on a back road getting bad notices?

She never killed the ones who couldn't answer,
had no interest in death or dying,
wanted only to make a living

and for a woman supporting herself
it wasn't easy. No, the men
who couldn't answer her riddles

just walked off saying—"Oh that's dumb,"—
until Oedipus took the whole thing
seriously. The first to come

with some wit, but over-proud and
so sure he'd found the answer
he never listened as she warned:

"You don't know as much as you think
this is only the first of a string
of right answers that will turn out wrong."

No, he just put her eyes out quickly
and finished her off, eager
to get down the road to Thebes.

Nikki Giovanni

Forced Retirement

all problems being
as personal as they are
have to be largely
of our own making

i know i'm unhappy
most of the time
nothing an overdose
of sex won't cure of course
but since i'm responsible
i barely have an average
intake

on the other hand
i'm acutely aware
there are those suffering
from the opposite affliction

some people die of obesity
while others starve to death
some commit suicide
because they are bored
others because of pressure
the new noun is as elusive
as the old

granting problems coming
from within
are no less painful
than those out of our hands

i never really do worry
about atomic destruction
of the universe

though i can be quite vexed
that Namath and Ali don't retire
my father has to
and though he's never made a million
or even hundreds of thousands
he too enjoys his work
and is good at it
but more   goes
even when he doesn't
feel like it

people fear boredom
not because they are bored
rather more from fear
of boring
though minds are either sharp
or dull
and bodies available
or not
and there's something else
that's never wrong
though never quite right
either

i've always thought the beautiful
are as pitiful
as the ugly
but the average is no guarantee
of happiness

i've always wandered a bit
not knowing if this is a function
of creeping menopause
or incipient loneliness
i no longer correct my habits

nothing makes sense
if we are just a collection of genes
on a freudian altar to the species

i don't like those theories
telling me why i feel as i do
behaviorisms never made sense
outside feeling

i could say i am black female
and bright
in a white male mediocre world
but that hardly explains why
i sit on the beaches of st croix
feeling so abandoned.

Crutches

it's not the crutches we decry
it's the need to move forward
though we haven't the strength

women aren't allowed to need
so they develop rituals
since we all know working hands idle
the devil
women aren't supposed to be strong
so they develop social smiles
and secret drinking problems
and female lovers whom they never touch
except in dreams

men are supposed to be strong
so they have heart attacks
and develop other women
who don't know their weaknesses
and hide their fears
behind male lovers
whom they religiously touch
each saturday morning on the basketball court
it's considered a sign of health doncha know
and they take such good care
of their bodies

i'm trying to say something about the human condition
maybe i should try again

if you broke an arm or leg
a crutch would be a sign of courage
people would sign your cast
and you could bravely explain
no it doesn't hurt—it just itches
but if you develop an itch
there are no salves to cover the area
in need of attention
and for whatever guilt may mean
we would feel guilty for trying
to assuage the discomfort
and even worse for needing the aid
i really want to say something about all of us
am   i   shouting   i want you to hear me

emotional falls always are

the worst
and there are no crutches
to swing back on

Beckian Fritz Goldberg

Eros in His Striped Shirt

I decided to stop
meeting my demons, detoured
that street, that orchard full of yellow
spheres that never revolved, and went
around the stairs where—

This is delicate.
There are things you should not say
because you love someone.

I woke many nights. The last
suddenly like a beat
in a drum: Demon *If. If*
with his black beard and his
brown coat, gazing down at
me from the stairs. How I followed him,

schoolgirl.
Do you imagine at night someone
going to bed the very moment
you are going to bed? Turning
out the light?
And isn't it so quiet you swear
the heart is telepathic.
Isn't it—

I came out of myself like fire
and went back in. We do
lose what we never had. Because

we imagine.
(A dangerous imagination, Mother said)

As if in a library—
as if on my naked shoulder—
they whisper *Yes, we are horses*
and offer the beggar's ride.
But I've done to me and I've done to me.
(Out of control, Husband said)

Now I'm on foot, dragging
the mind's clandestiny.
(You will meet the ministers
but not the Prince, *I Ching* said)
Night's floored to the metal,
ruinous obsession. Flesh, beware—

to live is homesick.

My Husband's Bride

The past begins to move at night.
A white peony too open from the heat
catches a soft light in its hackles
a room away from where the body, lost
from sleep like the amorous stranger,
the mental America, sits
with a little vodka turning
the stares of guests
in the wedding album. I hear
another year rustle by like the night's
one car. I put my hand through
the bed's blind side.
He is with her again. The bride
smiling where her shadow's thrown
a black water she could walk.
It's a day like spring in January,
a bloom pinned to the chest
where the body's grown back

over its life. All around our house
couples have begun to die
of a mysterious unhappiness.
Their supper tables have thinned
to wire. Their touch like jars
where a little doubt flutters.
They have disproved equation
after equation that a woman
and man traveling time can get out
young again and promise everything.
But it is not hers now.
The bride's face is like the delicate
print of the face of my thumb,
the part of me I have lost
but lost to him.

Say

Tongue, what are you doing up there in space
among the tunnels of birds and the about-to-snow,
still as the blush on far fruit?

I stand with only breath in my jaws, the absurd
fur on which I cannot place even a
finger. Then it comes to me to say about
the weather, something, by which I mean. And
he says about the weather, and I some
thing about his coat, by which I mean

everything. But he lets it drop.
Everything, what are you doing out there,
out there? Come in
like salt. But at twilight cold red lilies

half undress the spheres
inside them. Crows are snipping *want want want*—
the neighbor's broom against the walk tears out
of a terrible throat

confessions. Each time I am near
him, my voice fades like a scent. And his eyes

say, What are you doing here?
Longing is tighter than anything.
    They fix to the air to the left
of my face, a black language. *And it
about him—he is what
by which I mean by.*

Hound and Leper

The madwoman in gloves
has let her hand blow open
through soily eyelets, and points
one finger at me across the street.
You're so ugly, she yells.
And in the tinny sunlight I glance
behind me hoping to see
the grotesque. *Where'd you get
such an ugly face?*
She approaches, her blue socks
in rings and a man's shoe
mouthing open at the toe.
I walk on straight and slowly
like my loved ones told me . . .

She shakes her fist as I pass.
A pigeon is whining in the palm tree
and some house with a passion vine
tangles to my left. Will she
follow me, my accuser:
Hash-haired, malty-breathed, eyes of
aluminum and string. At the bridge
she passes under and I
over the hard crease and quartz,
fossil bed of the river
whose mirror has walked. She's seen it,
the disfigurement of dream,

hound and leper in my face—
how flesh is always on
the scent of something, and the marrowy
suck of my eye is creating
symbiosis: Hunger and denial.

It is the one who does not love you
whom you finally believe. Tonight in that
drift before sleep, her voice
is his. On the ceiling, Eros rides
Psyche. I sleep disguised
as myself, my derelict.
Where'd you get that mouth? Christ.
Her eyes hidden behind her hand
mid-street. My no one.
My confessor. My lips are red iron.
I can't bear their secret.
I'd stuff them with dynamite
and run. Straight home,
like my loved ones said.

Stephanie Goldstein

At Night

Worries creep like insects
out from under my pillow
into my sleep.

I am in a drugstore, staring
at a six foot two inch
bottle without a cap

packed with blue and white capsules.
I ask the druggist,
"What's this?"

He takes my prescription
then points his swollen finger
at cards, cosmetics, and flowering plants.

"This brings out the color of that,"
he says, pointing
to red flowers and green leaves.

"Green," he says. This is bizarre,
I say to myself. "Yes," I say to him,
"but I don't understand,

I'm already on Methotrexate, Ansaid, Cytotec,
Now the doctor wants me on more?"
The druggist looks upset

while I'm still staring at the giant
bottle which has divided into three
smaller bottles with black caps.

They tip their caps and smile
like chauffeurs giving greetings.
They stand beside the long limousine.

The druggist, meanwhile, keeps repeating
the same thing. And I keep saying,
"What's green got to do with it?

How about my kidneys?" "Don't worry
about that," mutters the chauffeur
with a smile like a worm.

He holds the door open and croaks, "Get in."

Miriam Goodman

Poems from a Country House

Wooden Chair

She'll press me. I stay stiff-backed.
I reach my arms out, but don't unbend.
I won't change my position.
Her shifting disturbs me.
If truth drops with its awful weight,
I'll crack.

House Dirt

I am the milky cloud that settles
in her glass, curd of motion
and evaporating time. I am
the dust motes in the hiding air,
blackness that descends
and wears her out. Drops doubled
in the mirror, moisture on
the varnish of the wood, I want
to touch her and not be brushed away.

Pitcher

I purse my lips around
a clutch of wildflowers,
from mouth to swelling base,
a single line. She makes
the arrangement, I hold
it in place, with my great gift:
to stay as she sets me down.

Habits

Sunlight fills the front hall. She leaves the front door
open as if in this house she had no shame. There is nothing
unique about her foolishness; it's the passion of middle age for
youth, its own past youthfulness. In this retreat they rent, the
furnishings are plain. She longs to look at something beautiful.
But here there are muslin curtains with pinch pleats, emptied
whiskey bottles used for lamps.

The sun, rising behind the mountains, shines in their
bedroom window, and by each bed, symmetrically placed, a chair to
hold their extra things. By hers, the books and magazines; by
his, a blanket, set aside because of hot weather, or ready to be
used if it gets cold. When they make love, he stuffs his
underpants under his pillow, squirrels them away. She puts hers
on the chair with the nightgown she removes. Their nakedness had
been their achievement; without him, she thinks she will be
caught forever in her office clothes dismissive and abrupt.
Without her, he thinks he will again be the odd child, dodging
random cruelty by hiding and delay.

Here, among these things—a night table between
the twin beds, the vase of dusty cattails on the dresser, the
pink boudoir chair—they have learned something new. All their
impressions of each other have entered their open eyes and
stayed. She has borrowed his childhood habit of dressing a chair.
Their deerskin slippers wait by their beds. Who would guess
tomorrow she'd be leaving? The night table holds their
eyeglasses, water glasses, tissue box and lamp.

Lampshade

People always ask how I was made.
A woman, wanting cash, made me
with wild flowers,
pressed between vellum,
rigidified by hoops,
to have a shade, a mystery,
and something to advertise,
like the crinoline
she wore in high school
to make her hemline flare.

Then eyes went up her legs
to the dusky foyer of her skirt
but couldn't penetrate.
The light inside was never switched on, then.

Now she is cold and angry with herself
for giving in to lust
so now she can fix me—
calculate this small surprise—
a pocket of parchment,
into which she slides
petals like a snakeskin,
shed and rearranged,
and bearded grass.
She sews me up with gimp,
settles me upon a spindle
where I embrace, with distant
arms, the bulb.

Barn

They lock me now. I store their blades
and snaths, their summer car. A visitor
will raise the latch and look. I listen
back. The past churns up in me,
settles like a scattering of dust.

I see how bright it is out there.
Sun bales me, bundles me in stripes.
Trees leave a shadowed vagueness
on my roof. My walls are boards
nailed end to end. The lengths

are parting at the join. It's true,
I've lasted a long time. It comforts
them, my being here. They put
an "old" before my name. I dream
of falling in or catching flame.

Braided Rug

I hold myself so tightly coiled,
my many pasts so intertwined,
I can't remember how I came to be.
I submit to what you make of me,
the patterns you discern,
the motifs you assign.

I'm your antique. My care
becomes your job. Don't
worry, I won't ask a thing.
Before I come apart, I'd fray.
You'll want me less, eventually.
You'll put me more and more away.
Let me lie down.
I would be as I was,
rags in my maker's hands

Valerie Graham

You Know

the way it is in fall, the moon a diamond
disc, collected, poised to polish
granite. Windows glinting squared
moons, your shadow cavernous
before you, no stars—the sky so

white—and every breath a knife
blade in your throat. Crickets
scratch up silver, mist
merges to a lake in swayed
light. Starts as a scrimmed

backdrop, burgeons, bellies,
swells. Dare you
walk? You could lose
your legs, feet down among
summer's dead

fireflies and seeds of uncut
orchard grass. The stuff of
myth: Persephone. Again. The Ice
Queen in her cave unkissed and you falling
in. You know the way.

Anne Haines

Catching the Scent

Summer evenings, I was put
to bed before dark. I'd kneel
on the mattress to look out the window
and watch my mother talking
to the neighbor across the fence,
standing near the roses that bloomed
though we never took care of them.
The evening light was long and soft
falling across the lawn.
I couldn't hear my mother's voice
and she didn't turn to see me
watching. That summer
I began to see her life as separate
from mine,
         in long light, among roses.
Later, I'd wake in the dark
and lift my face into night air,
the insistent breeze of far places.
At the edge of town cars hummed
on the speedway, their sound
punctuated by the rasp of cicadas
calling to each other.
             In moonglow
and in half-sleep, I imagine
the night as an open place
stretching out around me.
I cannot see the roses
but smell them blooming
on dark wind.

Vanessa Haley

Gangrene

You were ready to die, embarrassed that your four
grown daughters had to help you to the bathroom,
that your gangrenous foot, swollen and dark,
with which you would not part, filled the room
with a smell I cannot place—the fox along the side
of the road in spring I slowed down to see—its
delicate, pointed face of death.
Diabetes took your sight when you were still
a young woman, the age I am now, though you pretended
to see as blindness settled in, memorizing the house
so no one would know your life was a series of steps
and turns, counting potatoes and jars of pears
in the pantry, miraculously never burning yourself
or falling. You lived in darkness so long
it was your second home, and even blind,
kept an immaculate house, feeling walnut tables
and counter tops for dust or crumbs, your hands
fanning out their small shapes, like leaves
on the yellow ginkgo tree glowing in the front
yard the day we all came back to select a remembrance.
I took that old hurricane lamp, one you read by
perhaps many years ago. Now I light it when a storm
brings down the power lines and I am left
stumbling through my own house, thinking of you,
the stone-blind woman I never knew,
who fingered my Sunday dress and blonde hair
when I was just a girl, frightened by the intimacy

of your touch. And the photograph of your favorite
daughter, the only child you outlived, my father's sister,
the one I resemble, I am told, and her six pairs
of high heels that you faithfully polished
for thirty-two years and lined up neatly
on the closet floor, as though she might come back
one day and take you ashore to the other side of blindness.

Miss Gee Meets W. H. Auden in Heaven

Women don't fantasize about a leathery toad
like the Vicar of Saint Aloysius, nor are our dreams
full of phallic symbols. The "lowered horn"
was too much, really, and the fields of corn—
well, you've put too much stock in Freud. It seems
you came to hasty conclusions about me,
as most people did—that I must be lonely
without a husband, a spinster, repressed,
certain that at church I confessed
to fears of temptation and prayed to remain
celibate. My lover was invisible to everyone.
For more than thirty years we sustained
a loving relationship. Your opinion
should at least have been swayed by your own
proclivities, but you condoned the town's
provinciality and failed to see my love
for another woman. Often, after she died,
I held a pair of her worn-smooth winter gloves
and touched my face with them, lightly, closing my
eyes, imagining her soothing hands, the scent of her,
the light caresses on my neck. One November
when we took a meandering ride on a back
road and stopped next to a meadow where a cluster
of elms held a congregation of crows, I had a wish
that when they startled from the trees, as black
and shimmering as Margaret's hair, and vanished
into a blue abyss, we could assume the perfect

posture of winged things, and ascend too.
In the open field, we embraced and kissed
and felt no shame. What we hide as women
in an opalescent heart, a pearl lodged
in our throats like a word we can't say, an ornate
fish bone . . . the secret of distinct trembling. A mirage
of two swans drifting across a polished lake
repeats itself to me, in that intangible
place only Margaret knew. There were no clues
except exclusion. Unobtrusive, we
scrutinized astonishment
wherever we found it:
in the profusion of blooms our dogwoods gave,
in a box turtle's parquet shell abandoned
on the forest floor. We tipped it to release
the body's memory. Or in the mole, making
a home from the dark and lonely pursuits
of obscured vision, its traceries in the grass
scattered like blind hope for light's tolerance.

Marie Harris

Trial Separation

She rented a little windblown house with two bedrooms and a
single tree in the back yard onto which every morning evening
grosbeaks descended like a brief squall. She bought new sleeping
bags and a green record player for her sons. She changed her brand
of dish liquid to one that smelled exactly like fresh peaches and
found a part time job reading the papers of a freshman science
fiction class. She invited a younger man to dinner. One afternoon
a painter came by and said he had always loved her. A visiting
poet and her lover spent an evening in the bathtub. Her friends
told her she looked wonderful. By late spring her husband took to
calling at odd hours to talk about himself and ask her to come
home. It was time, he said. She packed up, drove the eight miles
to a house where the kitchen had been painted too yellow and his
study a cold shade of blue. When she turned down their bed she
found a stain on the sheet.

Lola Haskins

Message

Don't you see, there were limits
even to this, places where I could not
follow: into the heart of wood,
beyond the killing singing power line.

The Shoes

They were wine suede with just a thin strap
across the ankle. Sometimes I could tell
they were wrong, but I didn't care.
I wore them with everything. When they began

to sag, it was only a little at first, like shoulders
at the end of the day, and it didn't matter
that my feet slid extra with each step. I pulled the strap
tighter. It bit a new hole. Then their color

began to turn sad and stains to rise up their sides.
Water markings, the wavy outlines of tears. And
underneath how thin they grew, how easily small stones
would bruise. A heel came loose. I nailed it back.

But the nail head worked through to my bare heel and
every left step pained. My walk lop-sided to a limp.
I took the shoes downtown. The aproned cobbler turned
one over, gave it back. *These are too far gone,* he said.

Buy yourself some new shoes, he said. The sun
hit the floor like new leather, hard and raw.

Lyn Hejinian
and Leslie Scalapino

Excerpts from *Sight*

This conscious attempt to see is producing sensations of
searching
As in a museum—or walking off balance, hurrying forward
in order to compensate for the weight of my eyes and even then
leaning—I am drawn from one thing to another
(LH)

pool of lagoon moving
  doesn't occur

its rim's in the newspaper even.
  it's completely clear with a mountain in it. and
  not generating memory. it's *just* memory actually.
  won't accept his bullying however promulgated by
  them ever
(LS)

But I accept a greeting at a place I've never seen, leaning
toward the wind, as someone moving forward is coming to mind—
and the moment itself is being remembered at the same instant,
with the event recognized
At a beach with breakers at it in the absence of whatever
there is between anything and me
(LH)

Thin silver disc moon shredded at the bottom edge is
  seen in late day. it has a fringe that's shredded and
  seen a few days ago. But not memory as a function to
  see.

One's seeing it today when it has occurred really before,
and not using memory for it.
   Memory occurs on its own.
   One's seeing it anyway, as if in or by forgetting,
   rather than at the time of its occurring
     It occurs then but is seen
     now on blue evening which doesn't exist.
   I only remember it later, but am seeing it by forgetting
     later and while it's occurring
   Silver moon disc in blue occurs in the separation
(LS)

When our movement is due to that of the window
And then this seeing is not a silent proceeding
I've hung a man in the upper branches of the tree and he's
expected to sing to me
But in the interval between that sight and this expectation
(and the spectre prolongs this interval) I change my memory, and
the sight to which I've referred (in memory) recurs as another
sight

   The faster we go, the nearer we are to the trees
(LH)

The shredding at the lower rim of disc of
   moon is in the separation
   by its not being remembered when it's happening

   I have to remember its event
   of occurring then but is seen now
     to have fights inside
(of others)
     though it exists
(LS)

Lyn Hejinian: Leslie Scalapino and I began this collaboration in early 1993; what appears here is the very beginning of the work, and it was written before the collaboration had a title, although the sections do conform to the two "rules" we agreed upon, namely, that we would write about things seen, and that each "poem" or "installment" or "response" or "section" (we've referred to the parts in all of those terms) would consist of twos—two paragraphs, a paragraph and a stanza, two stanzas, two words, two pages, two sentences, two "takes" (to use film vocabulary), or any other conceivable manifestation of biocular (binocular) and stereoptical perceiving. For me, the use of twos contributes to the underlying logic that sustains the writing, since it rhymes with the fact that we are two people seeing, two people writing, we each have two eyes, and we are trying to peer at both thing and word, with the double point of view implicit in that, with perceptions simultaneously immediate and mediate, in time and out of time, and so forth. I don't remember when we added the title, "Sight," but the need for one may very well have been prompted by the invitation to publish a part of the collaboration in *Sojourner*.

In responding to that invitation, I wrote to Ruth Lepson that "I have sometimes thought that feminists have either resisted or missed what experimental writing offers toward subverting hegemonic, patriarchal control over the means of knowing. Poetry is a field of thought and information, and new modes of writing it provide not just new thoughts but also new ways of thinking." A writing collaboration increases one's chances and options for finding new things and new ways to think and see.

One of the other reasons I am so interested in collaborations is that the collaborative process invites and insists that one acknowledge the social impetus and impact of writing. One seems literally to go "out of one's way" to speak to one's fellow writer, and this applies a kind of perceptual pressure to the work. It is always saying, "Do you see what I mean?" and in order for the other to answer, "Yes, go on, I follow you," one must write very carefully and very clearly. This search for "clarity" is another rhyme with our theme—sight is difficult when conditions are obscure.

Some of our writing is, at least at first reading, perhaps "strange." Strangeness is not at all the same as obscurity. Strangeness restores unusualness to familiar things—making them unfamiliar so that they come to our attention again and thus become visible. This is not a new idea—Tolstoy used "defamiliarization techniques" in his writing, for example (as when Natasha, in *War and Peace,* goes to the opera for the first time and we see it from her point of view, as a bunch of gesticulating fat people belting out foreign songs in front of painted cardboard).

Although neither collaborations nor strangeness are feminist strategies per se, feminism can make use of them. The collaborative process redefines the ego in the course of redefining the nature of authorship. In collaborating, we surrender power, forget our autonomous selfhood, and are free from narcissistic inhibitions. We are we—which is a great relief when one is so frequently an "I" and is bullied and supervised as such, whether male or female.

The "we" of collaborations is not the we of a gang; instead it can be the we of supervention, the we of surprise.

Leslie Scalapino: Our collaboration arose at Lyn Hejinian's suggestion; I've never collaborated before. We chose a form, working in pairs; and a theme, of sight. We send each other our responses, revising so far only slightly but with the thought of editing later at the conclusion of this cumulative work, which has no determined end (we loosely set a 30–page limit, but then decided to continue at will). The project is feminist, I suppose, in sometimes raising issues of social seeing that creates boundaries of gender.

As to the line "Thin silver disc moon shredded at the bottom edge is": The "beauty" of the line has to do with seeing as making distinctions that see one's "seeing as beauty," part of a dialogue between "inner" seeing and that which is "socially articulated," between casual conversation as in letters of two correspondents and "transgressing" the "boundary guard" into "poem/prose."

Jan Heller Levi

Tuscarora

Everything shifts: orange hills,
pale hills, Nevada hills.
Everything shifts into valleys
of light . . .

Morning interrupts the night.
A fragment from the diary of a woman artist:
"Again, I feel as I used to when the children were sick.
I stayed closely by them, did everything for them,
did not even think about my own work.
Tending them back to health.
This glorious feeling then of reconquest:
they will stay.
I shall keep them."

I hold a young goat in my arms.
Her thin, crooked legs,
like broken pencils, twitch
and beg for the ground.
Released, she runs back to the shed,
graceful again,
the dry earth echoing beneath her hooves.
I feel the vibration in my toes.

My father walked forever down a hall,
to me, forever waiting by a nurses' station.
What is it, I said.
They can't save your mother
and he fell into my arms and I

into his Oh Dad, oh dad, and together
we sailed away
while upstairs in surgery
woman overboard the doctors called a year too late.

Hills, valleys, invisible ocean . . .
The sun sets a hundred different ways behind this ghost town.
Sick moon rises, drips
like a candle into me;
I harden like wax.
I think of children leaning forward with warm, empty breasts,
tending to death those they could not tend to health,
those who could not stay, all the mothers
we could not keep forever.

Fanny Howe

Crossing Out

Gum up the works, girls,
then run from the mess as fast as you can.

Know why? No, why.

Down a pale incline rushing they went.

It was night and their own smiling
stopped them with their hands.

Brambles, silhouettes of nutshells, liquidambar,
fern dainties pressed on the aquarian blue.

Tell us if we're free!

Yes, you have found the page outdoors.
Therefore it's all yours. It's not rage

urging on a springlet in the woods,
or waterballs rolling through electromagnetic fields,

the hiss of sand over sand. . . . No,
it's mini-flames of pleasure hidden in your glands.

Like a map twisted in a tree top
—the shapes all doggy and cone-dripping—

your bill of freedom from day one.

Lynne Hugo

Small Power

I know how these things go:

he will give me his names, one
at a time, the first

like a vase, the last like water
in it, ready for what may be

given, later, the fragile bud
of his middle name, the more strange

the better the vulnerability
of the story, as though he wrote

on a small white card and set it
by the bloom in a vase of fresh

water. I never forget
a middle name, its small power

a dried flower saved
in a drawer, proving something,

and I am not sorry then,
though I never tell my own.

Julie Kalendek

No part of the hand was hungry

feeling over the window ledge
but it reached in and came back with
list upon list of amusing skills.

For sport they played with the idea
of the glamorous parts of the negligee,
a crack to the body's foundation.

Just keep walking she told herself.

Everyone made an issue over her
not liking to be touched
and none of them touched her and one

said is it something you would like

to talk about. As he continued to
enumerate the exact locations
of the anatomical heart. To enucleate

his own. Sickening marks of defeat.
She saw something in there.
And no one was prepared to fight
for anything.

Kathryn Kirkpatrick

Class

For my high school graduation
we went to the Western Sizzler
where my father, telling no one,
had reserved a private room.

He never believed in his own kindness,
and so he said nothing when I chose
a regular table. I was ashamed.
My boyfriend usually ate
at the Steak and Ale.

My family had no debts. No stocks either.
Just the slow rise of savings account
like water from a ceiling leak
into a rusty can.

But there were no leaks,
everything steadily tended
through long days of honest work
which left us at the end
of it all with only enough
for the chopped sirloin platter
and a room that stood empty
because we never arrived.

Stephanie Koufman

Violins tickling

Morning glories pleasure for a day
    Crickets remind her to breathe
Remind her to breathe.

After seeing
After the ears sketch
A slippery stroke
Nothing is as if,
Out of order
Or winds waffle
Pulls the body invisible

The soil, as moist as the hand
Squeezed
Leaving an imprint thick
    As the shadows' foam
On the roof top

I remember the voice distinctly
I interviewed him in sleep
Citgo sign flash,
Blemished and full of fire

She was
Pigeon holed and diagnosed
Patterns of trust along the fluorescent stream
Bind her, bundle blind thoughts.
Replace it all with peripheral starfish,
Morning glories and cherries plump.

I walk with a baby on my back
Wide-eyed
Not missing but yearning
For the first sip of ocean coffee.

Ruth Lepson

October 7, 1994

for Sally Sedgwick

The shadows of the bicycles are so sharp
on the yellowing brick path,
the yellow mums under the lamplight so
gold, as golden as the air
as her soul rose from her body.

The moon is cut in half.
The leaves of the locust tree, turned
mustard yellow, a sophisticated color,
chastise me, like an old lover—
your thoughts are sophistry, they say,

the truth is, Sally died today.

Remembering Emily Dickinson,
whom Sally loved to read, I dream
Sally's heart is a large heart
in the carriage of her body,
and horses rush it away.

They were gliding

They were gliding down the river,
I remember.
He leaned toward the turquoise water,
would not tell her what he wanted.
She tried hard to read the paper,
I remember,
she was tired,
couldn't read the Sunday paper,
couldn't smile or reach his hand.
Worried, he would tip the boat a little,
he would tip it without warning.
Only she fell in, remember,
freezing water, creatures under.
Caught in seaweed, I remember.
She was grateful when he saved her.
She was shaking,
he was better,
I remember.

Denise Levertov

Arctic Spring

The polar she-bear, dirty ivory
against the blue-white steep
slope of ice
rolls and slides like a cub,
happy to stretch cramped limbs after four
months in the stuffy den;
but quickly lopes
upward with toed-in undulant grace
back to the bleating summons
of three new bears, their first time out,
hind feet still in the tunnel,
black astonished eyes regarding
their mother at play, black noses
twitching, smelling
strange wonders of air and light.

Lyn Lifshin

The Child We Won't Have Is Crowding Us in the Front

seat of the Riviera
taking all the air
up, howling so the
light thru the maples
goes away. When I
try to move toward
you, it bops me in
the stomach, the car
veers toward the
edge. With the baby's
arm thrashing you
can't begin to try
to lip read. A torn
branch slashes thru
rolled down glass.
I give up writing
for an even bigger
illusion, stop
dancing to cook
and bear this child.
I never knew so much
of me could feel like
feet that had danced

7 hours every day
imprisoned in
stirrups, waiting
for what won't come

Curling on the Bottom of My Mother's Bed

as she would
on mine in
different houses,
bring me iced tea
at midnight or
cold chicken we'd
devour with our
fingers after
a date. I don't
think she minded
having to take
my arm in dark
restaurants
or crossing the
street, a good
reason to touch
me as she does
more freely now
as light in June
starts shriveling.
We whisper to
each other these
past 41 days we
haven't been apart,
like new lovers
who feel what
they have so rare
they can't bear
to sleep apart

Margo Lockwood

Bookshop in Winter

My cold sandwich sits on books,
the library stacked since yesterday
bought from a retired schoolteacher.
The turret of my open thermos
makes my desk a steamship.

In the folds of my jacket
a little warmth eddies out
as I bend and hoist book boxes
and the radio keens Schubert,
von Weber, Bloch.

Angelic pinions
on plate glass broken twice,
sweep icily along the edge of my outlook.

Two long Christmas weekends without the heat
create the crystals on the glass.
They take hours to dissolve. The cold discomfort
worth it if my thoughts lighten.

Pain is less if its compass is short . . .
Dickinson or Donne? I cross
the floor and pass to the backroom
where poetry shelves in the dark
light up. The gilding reflects
snowdrifts out back.

In Trinity College's long-windowed
library, a bibliophile showed me
how gold leaf in the titles made them
legible one gray Irish afternoon.

I had only to scan the Green outside,
the black cobbles under rain
to see the truth of his lecture.
Dark afternoons cut short
the hours scholars keep.

My long ago love affairs keep
to themselves in dark books,
the gold leaf of my attention
fitfully ruffling its pages.

Audre Lorde

Dahomey

In spite of the fire's heat
the tongs can fetch it.

It was in Abomey that I felt
the full blood of my fathers' wars
and where I found my mother
Seboulisa
standing with outstretched palms hip high
one breast eaten away by worms of sorrow
magic stones resting upon her fingers
dry as a cough.

In the dooryard of the brass workers
four women joined together dying their cloth
mock Eshu's iron quiver
standing erect and flamingly familiar
in their dooryard
mute as a porcupine in a forest of lead
In the courtyard of the cloth workers
other brothers and nephews
are stitching bright tapestries
into tales of blood.

Thunder is a woman with braided hair
spelling the fas of Shango
asleep between sacred pythons
that cannot read

nor eat the ritual offerings
of the Asein.*
My throat in the panther's lair
is unresisting.

Bearing two drums on my head I speak
whatever language is needed
to sharpen the knives of my tongue
the snake is aware although sleeping
under my blood
since I am a woman whether or not
you are against me
I will braid my hair
even
in the seasons of rain.

* Iron shrines at crossroads honoring the dead.

Ruth Maassen

Confessions of a Pisciphobe

Spiders don't faze me, mice, bats, no problem, but fish—
the single time I had hysterics I'd happened on
five plump perch on our kitchen counter—a safe place,
I'd thought till then—how could my mother so betray me?
Their tails were aligned, and the red vacancies
where their heads had been. They were hollowed out
by someone deft with a knife. I buried my head in a chair
and screamed and couldn't stop screaming. Alewife die-offs
in Lake Michigan had left their mark. You'd finally
get to the Lake—all that water sparkling before you—
but between you and it, windows of shining, stinking fish.
You'd barely save yourself from squishing one with bare toes,
then wade out and have one drift under your chin. Lake vacations
were one long shudder, with boys cleaning their catch
at scale-encrusted tables out behind the cottages.
Even away from the water, salmon on platters jumped
out of magazines (I hastily turned the page) and jars
of pickled herring sprang from the cheese shelves.
Later, I confessed my weakness to lovers, then lived in fear
I'd find a fish in my bed, under the covers down near my feet,
put there to improve my character. I married the last one
because I was sure he'd never do such a thing, in fact
he's so eager to protect me it perversely makes me almost
want to look. Fate decreed we move to Gloucester, which lives
for fish. My office is set amid dead fish in plastic crates,
wheeled gray bins, semi trailers, whole container ships full.
Across the street they process fish waste into mink food—

there's some satisfaction in that dripping stench
being transformed into pelts for the wealthy, but I find
fish pieces wet on the pavement, or whole ones driven over
until they're flat and dingy as newsprint. I look at them
with hardly a jolt, and drive with eyes only slightly blurred
behind pickups full of heads and tails bouncing. Still,
to turn a corner and see all those black eyes staring—
I have to admit fish are beautiful, at least unputrefied,
or alive in their all-muscle surges through water or air,
but please don't take me to an aquarium, don't take me
diving down to where they'd hold me in in their gaze.

Michelle M. Maihiot

Playing Fields

and the homogenous roar of the bleachers,
same red leaves on the same tree,
same slap—back echo with each call—
"second and four!", whatever.

Precision like a goose-stepping parade,
I want to be as seasonal, as predictable,
as timed as foliage.

With each pill I try to cycle this mind,
manipulate currents in a poorly planned electrical dam:
energy building for something profound and illuminating
like lightning.

I want to be who they think of when they say,
"Some things never change."
I want to walk the paths of myself, seasonally,
and know which leaves turn first, which trees have died.

Jennifer Markell

The Veterinary Student

They told her she would have to kill the dog.
For months she had pleaded, written letters,
attached photos of the Dalai Lama.

Now she forces herself to touch the dog's ear,
remembering her own hand, hand of the un-maker
remembering this is just a dog and not
a third world nation.

The needle slides into a thicket of fur. She watches
the brown eye slip into its pale socket and disappear.
She strokes the ear, not to calm him
but to keep herself from falling.

The ear is soft, not unlike other soft things
she has touched, the egg of a bluebird
and other things that give way under pressure.

Suzanne Matson

The Beach

The boy and the girl toss the white ball
in the blue sea,
the blue sea glistens
the white ball—*pong* against fists—
glistens
as do the bodies of the children
wild as alphabet letters.
They each overthrow the ball
shouting with pleasure at the strength of their inaccuracies.

The young men
hit the ball
to each other
on the hard-packed
margin of sand
before the sea.
They work their
crisp volley faster
and faster until
they have some-
thing between them
as hard and pre-
cise as a thigh
muscle, as clear
as a perfect
understanding.

The women lie on the beach like
unshelled mollusks. They lie
on the beach and turn heavily
in the glaucous mirror of all the gazes
they have turned inward since
the ball left their hands for good and they held cupfuls
of themselves instead to be measured against the heaviness
of a world turned inner, swelling from their own and
the world's excess which everywhere began cutting fine red patterns
into the flesh.

Worry

When worry moved in it clasped itself
like a boss's large hand amiable at the back
of the neck, one finger pointing to the base
of the skull, the others splayed toward the slope
the shoulder makes. With worry hooked
there so that the head not quite rested against it,
the head was suddenly aware of its own weight,
like a bloom on a too-thin stem,
wagging askew of the plumb line that falls from crown
to footsole. Then walking became
walking with the head,
holding it as you hold a part-time job,
that extra obligation, that due you pay
to the guiding avuncular palm facing you
toward your future.

Linda McCarriston

Kitchen Terrarium

I

No, not much, the old song
travels back to me from memory,
from when I was your age,
I don't want my arms around you,
I don't bless the day I found you,
no, not much. Old standards,
tender and sad, surprise me,
reminding me of you, the child
I miss more than ever I missed
a lover. Everywhere are brown-
haired boys in jeans. Everywhere
are mothers who barely notice
as the schoolbus stops, starts up
with its long sigh, and the kids
bang in, their voices still running
at bus-din pitch, the dog leaping
hip-high beside them, to hit
the first flat surface with a stew
of papers and books. You aren't
here, upending my kitchen, hungry
and loud. You won't go off to play
with friends, won't come back
these narrowing afternoons at dusk
as you have all the Octobers,
each of which, like single afternoons
heading toward this one, has borne

more dark than the last, its think light
bullied down to this darkest October.
Soon we'll set the clocks back.
I dread it—the black outside the windows,
each window a mirror reflecting
empty space, your face not here,
intent over paper, your body
not boogeying by, preoccupied, nothing
of you here, not even your place,
when I turn to set plates on the table.

II

All day in front of the judge
and before we began, I knew the outcome.
I wore a dress. I presented myself as
a lady—the least and easiest
of selves, but there the best that is said
of a woman, and the face that requires
no reprisal. Your father the doctor,
vested in white, had come to say
he was ready. And with him the lawyer,
making truth out of lies and money.
All day their expert testimony fell
—words of strangers, words from books
written by governors for the sake
of governors—like bombs on the city
that was your whole life with me,
childhood: its thousand streets, each
with its hundred houses, each of these
with its many rooms, its multifold
ordered contents built up by love's
long attentions over years. But in
the Protectorate of Legitimacy, the sword
was hanging—and I knew it—
whetted on the righteous idea.

When the judge rose, in the gown
of a woman, to speak his decision, I rose
in my blood's roar, straining to hear.
The part he read straight at me
was where he called you *a man:* by dictum

the great excision had begun, the boy
from the woman. In my mind's eye
I saw you outside the courthouse
partway up a tree, where you'd climbed
to see if parallel streets couldn't meet
on some far horizon. A sixth grade boy,
four foot nine, you still gave
turns to the teddies you slept with.
it might have been the Judgment of Solomon,
but the judge was not wise. He halved
the child, and the false mother gloated
—thumbs up—at the glad decree.
Had I hoped something different would happen
there, blind stone the only woman in the
chamber besides me? Did I think he would
want you whole, this judge, halved,
like the rest—he cannot remember it—
and hardened into a man?

III

Today at the kitchen table I write
the one letter your father permits

each week. Then I write postcards
I can't send yet. I'm ahead of myself,
a backlog of longing for even

the least hello: *Are you ready
for skiing?* I enthuse on the back
of the photo—a swirl of white

at the knees of the red-suited
athlete, as if it were you
in the picture, as if I, not there

on the slope beside you, were just
out of sight, cheering, making

the paper memory. In fact, it's still
only October. You're still only

a boy, and your father is by you now,
instructing. He takes you to town.
You get new skis. The season ticket,

the flashy gear. He takes you for walks
and shows you the husk of, say, milkweed,
the alien, gestative thing. You go

with him to the high ground we found,
the place you peopled with Indians,
and he points out the elm that dominates

that splendid, open space: a *winner,*
not a *loser* around. He takes you

to dine.

       But when you phone me

your voice is hollow: *There's nobody home,*
just the housekeeper. There's everything
here, but it's empty. There isn't

a kitchen. Axis Mundi of the Lesser World,
I sit in it as you left it, the heat
from the cookstove, the grain of the
table under my hand less palpable

to my own flesh than your sadness,
which fades against his gifts, his novitiate's
walks, but comes up, sudden, around you

like someone's old favorite turned loud
on the radio. Davey, if we are to sing of
or to each other in common terms, we must
use words long worn sore with meaning:

the rare soft moments of a hard lust, satisfied,
held up as love's highest figure. It is this
instruction into which you've been taken

to grow, like the moss and lichen
still alive here, that you gathered
and placed in the big glass jar on the table.
The glass is clear. From inside it must be

invisible, thus there must be an
Emperor of the Jar, a father, making
beside him a place for a son, to which

all of creation has been scaled: no trees
taller than a man to climb, no creatures
but pets and game, a mirror to look at and
walk upon, that he will tell you is *water*.

Helena Minton

Day Surgery Pre-op

Only two of us:
me and a young man from a halfway house.

He rubs his hands and whispers to himself;
on his lap a hairbrush and a bible.

I feel a tenderness towards him,
my friend in fear.
What if we don't wake up?

Other fears—
of heights, of flying—
are holidays compared to this.

That's why we startle
when the doors open
and in stride
young surgeons and nurses in blue scrubs,
chatting and laughing,
a Monday morning 8 am, so cheerful,

for a moment I remember
waking in the dark to hear my parents
call good night to friends,
their voices loosed on the street,
and closing my eyes,
happy things still went on while I slept.

Building the Compost

They talk about it for a year.

She wants to throw the rinds
behind the woodshed.

He says they need a frame
wrapped with chicken wire.

All summer she urges him to build,
not sure why she's so desperate.

Try it yourself, he says.

She walks to the workbench,
touches the tools,
her tears falling in the sawdust.

After the first frost
he builds a frame
as big as a walk-in closet.

It reminds her of the cage
where the witch locked Hansel
though she only imagines the bars.

It might be a fort,
a cupola where she can play with dolls,
a space to stand when she is angry.

She hammers horseshoe tacks
against the chicken wire.

Now, he thinks, she will be happy.

She finds herself moving
toward the thrift
of a woman in wartime,

saving scraps, starting seeds
for a victory garden.

Honor Moore

To Janet, on Galileo

Brecht's Galileo
Havermeyer Hall at Columbia, 1978

In the play about the first telescope, a man notes
    through Galileo's strange tube a moon's edge
not precise or sharp, but irregular, serrated.

    We face each other, two women friends, a small
table. Mouth ached to a smile, you begin: *The balance—*
    job, marriage, writing—it's stopped working. Passion

of discovery. Brecht argues such passion is true
    reason. You contemplate leaving a man. I
have left a man. A Hungarian restaurant. Sun

    not earth is center. Galileo argues
Copernicus. Priests argue heaven, Aristotle,
    crystal spheres that never move, and refuse to look

through the telescope. A man weeping. I cannot touch
    him. To comfort would keep me here. You speak of
leaving, feel abandoned. Fork lifted: *Perhaps I am*

    insatiable. Perhaps no one can love me
enough. Chicken paprikash, red cabbage, red wine. Gold
    light of April evening. Young women, young arms

around young men, whisper against university walls.
    Janet, women like us are caught in history,
a diaspora. A Leonard Woolf taking care is

not enough. We are not willing to forfeit
passion of love to have passion of work: We want both.
   A man's blunt body on blue sheets. Sweetness of

years. I leave, go on more alone. *Last night we talked*
   until light. Maybe it's time to part, is what
we came to. Janet, when I knew I had to leave the

   house where I'd lived seven years, I cried every
morning. If there were a child, perhaps I could not have
   left. Unrestricted inquiry, they warn him,

is dangerous for mankind. Galileo obsessed
   keeps eye to glass, night, Jupiter's four moons, hears
no warning. *If I leave, will anyone else ever*

   love me? Janet, I was in bed with my new
love kissing, and like a bolt I saw us, him, me
   seven years younger walking near the blue

river way downtown. Late lunch in a bar, blue sky fall
   vivid. I couldn't stop crying until I
reached the phone, called him, and I don't know if I cried for

   the loss of him, for the loss of a me who
could live with him, or for the loss of what I didn't
   know we'd lost until that night walking through snow

with someone else when ice air came in me like freezing
   breath and my mind began to know just I must
get out. A young man in the presence of his mentor:

   Galileo old, blind, silenced. The young man
asks, has he truly recanted? Yes. I have seen their
   instruments of torture, and my body fears

pain. Janet, I keep seeing: A woman forty stop
   painting: sanitariums, shock, drugs; her
daughter, after nine children, begins to write: cancer

   dead at fifty. I am her daughter. Yes, my
body fears. Galileo at the telescope: Three
   moons near Jupiter! I've proved Copernicus—

heaven moves! Writes his last at night, a prisoner, candle-
   lit, racing blindness. The young man smuggles it
free. Janet, we must risk our fear, this history. Perhaps

  we are insatiable. We walk, theatre
into cool night, the moon silver in a black sky, not
   serrated, but smooth. Perfect as a clear choice.

Blues

  I meet you again in public. I
walk toward you. People watch us. We are
   shaking hands. You touch my face: that smell,
you under a lamp, cowhide belt strapped
   tight around your arm, you pointing to
the bulbous flesh inflation near your
   shoulder: "Some women like to push the
needle in." Hand eight years older, still
   cool, smile diluted: I'm not sure if
it's because you're older or because
   my mind doesn't make you its magnetic
opposite anymore. Then "Hello
   Beautiful." Voice the same: You called me
that always after some sharp denial.
   It was, is pouring rain: I carry
your things downstairs. You are moving to
   another city. I am not. I
am weeping. Lamp, stack of manuscripts
   half-written: It is you I carry
down three stone flights. Was there any
   reason? Rain pours down the sides of
my face, and I am weeping: You
   would not take me with you. At the air-
port, you bought supper, said the duck that
   would not pass my throat would be good for
me. At the gate, "Goodbye Beautiful,
   keep in touch." I have not seen you for
eight years, and you are telling me you

have found a god who has calmed you. That
smell pours off your smile. I am pulled back—
　we are in public—my mind does not
make me your magnetic opposite—
　would you understand? You called four months
after the airport. I could not speak,
　hung up, threw a full glass, splattered
the white wall red. "Meet my bride," you'd said.
　Behind brown eyes a man paces out
nights pushed by a drug, that needle. I
　would not help you. I was twenty-three
and I loved you. The rain pours down my
　face, hides my crying. I am thirty:
Crying is anger and you did not
　understand. Magnet. Smell. Your gray hair
losing its clench. I am carrying
　you down stone stairs. It is dark, the last
I see you. I am weeping. I hold my self,
　hold her to me like an opposite,
a magnet. People watch us. You touch
　my face. It is a hot night at the
start of summer. We are shaking hands.

Rosario Morales

Old

Una

My mother at thirty was as luminous as a Puerto Rican dawn over the
cream sand beaches curving in and out and around the island. She was like
the moist fruit of the mango, like the fronds of the royal palm in the wind.
And I knew thirty was what I was going to be when I lost the skeleton I
wore, when I grew old, grew beautiful and free.

Dos

Skin
practicing to be old—
lining up, squaring off:
tracings
etchings
bas relief.

Look!
Over the blue
creek beds of my veins,
how the wrinkling
ripples sparkle
in the sun.

Tres

Que clase de vieja will I be when I knew none, grew up in New York City
when el Barrio was young like me and grandmothers grew in Puerto Rico,
when grandmothers were kept fresh in boxes of pictures under the bed and
became flesh only the summer I was going to be ten. We took a long sicken-

ing boat ride of a week to the magical landscape of Naranjito and on its one street I became "¡Mira! La hija de Lola, la de Mercedes." Abuela Mercedes was just like her photograph: large, cotton-wrapped, her breasts squared off onto her middle, hammocks of face dripping onto her chin, cushions of her melting into the brown floorboards. She smelled like maduros frying. And while the music from the jukebox across the street flies about her shoulders, crashes into the hibiscus bush, the guayaba, and as she stands imperturbable, solid, only her flesh giving way, I am comforted and afraid.

I cannot turn to my other grandmother. Abuela Rosario sat small, sat thin, sat straight and hard in a hard chair, knobbed hands on a knobbed stick. She beat one girl and ten boys into adulthood and my father beat me and I beat my babies and bit my hands and looked for knobs.

Cuatro

Crow's wings not feet—pinions
anchored to my eyes.
They spread in flight only
when I smile.
I smile.

Cinco

She warned me as she added sugar to the roasting coffee beans to blacken the brew, "Don't go out into the damp air, the cool night, after a day tostando cafe in an open pan over a hot fire, porque te vá a pámar." She said, "¡Cuidado, o te vá a pámar!" And she meant that the moment I hit the evening chill my warm skin would shrivel and wrinkle and ruck, a surrealer Rip Van Winkle. Only a moment would go by and I'd be old, old, older than old Doña Cornelia herself who always carefully wrapped a towel around her head and shoulders like a shawl before she left her burnt-sugar brown kitchen and stepped out beneath the banana leaves hiding the stars.

Seis

Maga was Jane's mother, my best friend's mother, was Alabama born, highborn, white as her hair, and even after twenty years in Puerto Rico couldn't speak Spanish and her a communist like her red-haired daughter, like her Puerto Rican son-in-law, like me.

I wanted to be like her when I grew old, I wanted the freedom to say what I liked, when I liked, to whom I liked, I wanted to pour Lapsang Souchong out of a china teapot into the endless afternoon and tell others what to do and how to do it. I wanted what I thought it felt like, sitting tall and highhanded, hair cut short and crisp, straight spine keeping the cops from stepping through the door to take her son-in-law César away, lean slacks bending. Lean hands reaching to grasp the garden weeds and smack the roots free of soil, grasping too at her daughter's home, her son, her time, and when Jane died, she reached for mine.

I couldn't give you that! But oh, Maga, will I sit as you sat, lonehanded, sipping tepid tea into the night?

Siete

Stop!
I don't want my scalp
   shining through a few thin hairs.

Don't want my neck skin to hang—
   neglected cobweb—in the corner of my chin.

Stop! at ruckling ruches of skin
   at soft sags,
     bags of tongue-tickling breast and belly,
   at my carved face.

No further.
Stop.

Ocho

No quiero morir

Robin Morgan

Damn You, Lady

(The Funky Double Sonnet
Tragicomic Lesbian Feminist Blues)

Damn you, lady, get out of my blood for good.
Your eyes, hair, laugh, your politics—erase
them—how your body's swift lewd grace once stood
beside me, how love lit your falcon face.

    Damn you, lady, I refuse to wail
    one moment longer so uncritically
    over you—as if I were a fool
    (or even incorrect politically).

Your gestures in quickliquid flow,
your voice, indigo as a violin's—
get out. Go, let my dreams sleep free
of you, your fragrance, words, songs, silences . . .

    Lovesick morons fail the revolution,
    mooning about while work needs to be done,
    and feminism's surely the solution
    to everything—except your being gone.

. . . the way you slept, woke, moved at midnight,
your antic grin that struck and blazed me glad
to be alive, the way you loved a fight
in a just cause. The way you drove me mad.

    Damn you, lady, I will not obsess
    one second more. Love's just a masquerade

at which we women, like men, can oppress
(an awkward truth we'd rather not parade).

But see? I have regained myself entire,
immune to you, asbestos to your fire.

Damn you, lady, I will yet live through
this memory, everywhere I turn, of you.

Kate Mullen

Thin-legged Lover

You always did like your men well hung
A thin-legged lover with arms outstretched
With ribs you could knit your fingers through
With a hollowed-out clavicle to dip your tongue in
With a hip-bone, poked out, to put your teeth into
With lips tight and tiny and never telling
With a jaw, carved, and forehead, heavy
Little-big hands calloused, hard, and clean
A man with a past, but little experience.
You always did like a man like that,
A man with scars that doesn't scar easily.
A thin-legged lover you can mount anytime, anywhere
And nail and nail and nail again.

Nina Nyhart

Vow

My mother is sometimes a summer hotel with cheerful blue and
white awnings, countless rooms and peeling white paint. This is
when she isn't a recently translated book, an unfinished card
game, or a scallop shell. Once she was a tractor and I knew I was
in trouble. My car broke down at the end of the causeway, I
stumbled back to the beach and to the mountains which might
have been her except she was describing them: *blue elephants.* She
called me her *pie* but it was she who fed me. I vowed never to be
like her, so foolish and metaphoric.

The Shoes

You can't just go into the shoestore and say
"I want those maroon shoes"—so you stop
at the cleaners. Waiting at the counter
you spot the two red maple leaves.
You're wondering what wayward tree dropped them
when Mrs. Tony slips them into your lapel.
It's a radiant fall day like
                            the ones years ago
when you worried about falling, what with one leg
shorter, the foot smaller. That's how you learned
about balance, imbalance, and how on a horse,
English saddle, the stirrups never hung right because

who could explain to a riding instructor, in English,
a thing so difficult, so private.
       It's October now,
leaves settle down to be kicked as in the old days,
but your left foot refused to do that, being
damaged itself. Meanwhile your right foot
was growing up correctly rushing out to give
a shove to any leaf or pebble foolish enough
to lie in its path.
       So when Mrs. Tony leans
across the counter to award the two red medals,
you notice the leaves aren't alike—one scarred,
the other larger. You both smile. You pivot,
head for the door and the store where you saw
those maroon shoes, in the window, glowing,
perfectly mismatched.

Playing the Part

  They came by the thousands into the square, eyeballs bulging
like Maybuds. It's all true, how they screamed, shouted, held
their young high for better viewing. I told them I hated fire, it
was my one real fear and I'd prefer the blade, so of course they
chose fire. To begin with, imagine the smoke, the wood being
damp. And then the heat closing in. Flames licking my toes and
ankles. I thought of the tongues of sheep and dogs back home
and the cold rush of streams in early spring and tried to be brave.
After all that pain and questioning, wouldn't you agree the only
thing to do was be brave? Wouldn't you say that the best course
was to try to be the most courageous person in the world?
Especially if you'd been waiting all your life for your turn?

Dzvinia Orlowsky

To Our Cosmeticians

1.

You want us to believe
there are only two kinds of women:
the Before
and the After.

In the Before Woman's life
it's always raining.
If you blow on her,
a parachute desperately opens.

She has no lips to speak of.

2.

Turn the page
and the After Woman appears.

She survives the hijacking of her heart.
She is the match-lit.

Her blush is the red of a bull's death.
Her hair bounces back for more.

She's been known to bite.

3.

If you ask me what season I am,
I would have to say late fall—
just at that time
when trees give up
and drop their leaves.

My best colors are:
file cabinet,
highway,
Ohio,

I wear them the way
the wind wears what it passes.

I like my meek mouth,
my no-grapes-on-the-stem look.
It makes me hirable.

4.

But thank you
for your day of beauty.

If I change my skin
it'll be gradual,

the rest of my life.

Molly Peacock

Dogged Persistence

Slowly an armchair turns on some sort of pedestal.
Oh Mother I know you will be in it!
I'm here in the fog and vapors, waiting
for you, clear little eyes behind hornrims,
to look up from your newspaper and stare out
at me, at me! But what a cold look you give.
You do not want to be bothered. *Mom,* I whisper,
it's me. You seem to have a reading lamp
—is that the little glow in the shrouded dimness?
"Don't bother me, Molly." Did you say that?
But I am searching for you! "Leave me alone."
Need, a child's need, a chill airless
panic instead of a mother as your chair
turns its back, and my hands dangle in the cold.
Where are you? You have to be out there somewhere.
I'll find you, I'll find you—how gray the sky is,
the sun a smothered 40–watt bulb behind clouds.
It is snowing, the sky decomposing,
each crystal, as we've all learned, individual,
as each person throughout millennia
is never replicated the same way,
yet out of the millions I will find the one
that is you. I have to go on.

The Raptor

Foolishly I'd imagined for you your mother's
death, but now you have your own. At home,
not in a nursing facility, your brother's
cheery, God-filled letters a comfort no one
(well, at least not I) would have predicted,
and me looking in on owlish you, cute
behind big glasses on your tiny head,
the growling, felled pet of your doctors. Acute,
inoperable cancer of the lung, although
you stopped smoking—not soon enough. I wonder
what I'm doing now that will create, under
unknown terms, my own death, far below
the high bright mark of your shadow, entirely
different from you—sharp as an owl's beak in your
awareness, yet drowsy as an owl. Will I
lie rattling the sidebar on my adult crib?
Will you die at home, without a bib,
after years of instructing me
which institution to slot you in?
Who knows what death I'll get exactly,
being daughterless, the line of begetting
neutralized, in hands beyond love.

Joyce Peseroff

After the Argument

Quiet here as the arsonist's noon—everyone in
for dinner, the marshal finding bottles
and waxed paper (he—or she—liked to watch)

in the country town where Edna Seavey's
stable burned, and the ell, blackening ropes
the widow used to feel her way to the privy.

I hiked Burnt Meadow Mountain's
summit ridge last fall, when maples flared
from the tip, like a struck match, and saw

the widow's Cape (auctioned to pay
for the nursing home) newly fitted with sliders
to dry another household's wash on winter days;

I saw the mourners at her grave. A woman who
in the Great Fire of Forty-Seven refused
evacuation, preferring to die, if necessary,

in her own rocking chair, Edna Seavey
uttered something shocking to the EMTs
who gurneyed her away, perhaps recalling

that October day when granite lisped to powder,
hay exploded in dry barns,
and standing trees spread fire root to root.

Carol Potter

White Hotel

for my grandmother

There is no house
like the house of your body
sitting in your new hotel. You are pinion,
wing, bone of air.
Nurses lift you from bed to
chair, chair
to bed. Down the hall, a woman
sings of a face only she remembers, in words
none of us understand.
My parents and I turn away.
We have heard nothing.
We have seen nothing.
There is no face
like your face
sitting in this white hotel.
We have taken everything else away, disassembled
your house, piece by piece . . . piano,
music box, bed. We tell you
this is your new home.
You are a white wing
in a white hotel, eyes
focusing on a bank
of unopened windows.
There is no sound
like the sound of that woman

singing at the other end of your hall.
We turn away.
We have seen nothing.
We have heard nothing.
There are just some things
I'd like to know, how all those years
you stayed alone. You look up
and tell me, "The babies are sleeping at home."
There is no hand
like your one hand waving
good-bye, Irene, making way
for somewhere else, tell me
one way to avoid lying down in this bed
and I will bring back
your green china cup I keep on my shelf.
I will bring back your cut-glass bowl, I keep
nothing inside it.

In the Upstairs Window

It was not all right when we got to your car and I saw the boxes
in the backseat, and you, laughing, asked me
did I want to go back to your house and help you pack.
You started talking about the weight of books, how much space
books take, how many boxes.
I want nothing to do with it.
Go home.
Pack it up.
Don't tell me it will still be the same.
Judith, there's a river through this landscape
and we ride away on it the way Cathy Fouloise's grandparents
rode their house down river during the flood of '55,
the two of them in the upstairs window
waving good-bye. I think of the house banging up on the bridge
abutment, the bridge washed out, shingles breaking loose
from the house. The front porch was stuck on shore
where the people stood watching; they stood
on the bank watching because there was nothing left they could do.

I keep wondering what it is we are all preparing for
going off to the new job in the next city—
it's difficult to refuse.
There's nobody to blame, and you laugh assuring me
that actually we will end up seeing each other
more than before. Sometimes it seems to me
we are each of us under some kind of obligation
to know how to walk away, how to shut the door,
how to leave the house empty,
to turn on our heels
as if we were all preparing for some grand good-bye
the way it comes in the dreams I have
where the world ends and I stand in the field
watching bright blossoms flare on the horizon.
Looking across that distance, in the dream, I am always wondering
how much time we have. There is a certain
resignation at that point, a strange new silence—
something peaceful, nothing more to be done.
I want nothing to do with this move.
Judith, for weeks I've been reading poetry manuscripts—
hundreds of poems, words, syllables—sound
on top of sound
and you can hear it on each page—
something palpable: the attempt
to bring back people gone—
places forgotten.
Sometimes I think all we're trying to do
with these reams of paper
is to stuff the mouth of this world, to stave it off—
those two lips, night and day—
the sound of the word
good-bye.

Martha Ramsey

Moving Out

You hear the scraping of my bicycle
on the stairwell as I climb,
so just as the door clicks open
you whistle a three-note call.

I'm back! I want to shout.
Did you miss me? But you're studying,
so I just wheel my bicycle in.

I feel alone here, coming from Eric's house
where I'll soon be living, where he and I
slept through dinner, hidden
in his shady room.

Some of your hair sticks up,
reddish, frail in the lamplight.
You too are a man I love
but I must not speak to you right now,
and I have not dared touch you
for the two years we've lived together.

In a few days I'll be leaving.
I am large with emotion,
like a heavy, smart girl
who has a crush on a shy boy.

Passing your chair tonight
I bend quickly to kiss your neck,
with secret face behind you,
as fierce on you as a mother.

❝ ❝ ❝

While I fill boxes, you read the paper
calmly on your bed.
I keep breaking into your room
with stories I've cut from magazines,
an old check to us from my father,
marked, "Paint and courage."

You read all cheerfully, with interest;
you say, *You save good things!*
I laugh, sitting on your bed,
and this is our way of saying goodbye.

We will forget
how we lived here,
how it was easy, often,
not to ask for too much;

the mornings we met in the kitchen
by chance, and shuffled around,
clumsy so near each other's
half-wet skin, and breath,

careful just to mumble things,
but sometimes grinning because we were
very pleased to see each other.

You with a tie holding up your bathrobe,
working through cereal, across the table . . .
I wanted a little something from you,
so I would say,
Have any dreams?

Jane Ransom

This Is Just a Fairy Tale

And it's for the ladies:
Beside Moses, a basket-case, Miriam
Waits. In the bull rushes.
Off with her outfit, and she's Europa
Getting it backwards
from Zeus.—Moses or Minos, Mary or Pasiphae,
It's the same rosy girl, same snow-white bull
Reforming, never reformed, remanifested
In each manifesto. Some guy always takes her.
Jesus or Jung or Mao Tse Tung. Let's memorize
mesmerization, study the angles as well as angels;
Let's fall apart and together like Tinkerbell Toys—
Come on, girls!—Let's abandon those boys.

Mary Kathleen Rayburn

A Hurdler Explains Her Reasons

I used to be a sprinter, running
straight down the cinder track.
The boys' eyes followed as
my legs ran by. And around the curve,
out of sight behind the storage shed
I'd stop, double over, and
heave to catch my breath.
Then, slick with sweat, slowly
walk back smiling at my friends.
One day someone left the hurdles
on the track. I ran anyway and
cleared that first hurdle as clean as
Wilma Rudolph jumping hedges on the way
to the store for her mama.
But my foot caught the top
of the next, my knees ground
into the cinders, my hip wrenched.
I cried without knowing it, shocked
to have fallen. It was timing, the coach said,
too many steps between hurdles.
So I began to practice—"step, step, step,
hurdle, land, step, step, step, hurdle,
land, step, step, step . . ."
Sometimes, I took down every hurdle,
leaving them like broken hearts in my wake.
Gradually, my feet forgot about running
straight and my body learned to hurdle.

My right leg stretched out,
a hunting dog pointing the way.
My left leg up and out to the side,
bent back like some crazy chicken wing.
The 'S' curve that traveled from my hips
to my head as I cleared each hurdle.
And underneath was always the rhythm.
Sometimes, I jumped an invisible hurdle
at the end of the course before
I stopped and knew that it was over.
Why jump hurdles when I could run
straight down the track? You should
ask my arms, my legs—my body.

Monica Raymond

Crossing the River

The river is black jelly, thrilled with reflections.
You insist like a child, only firmer. "But it is one
of my favorite things to do!" Surface lights
flap like a swimmer's legs, trace of what was swallowed,
    scissoring.
Remember, they seem to say, as if we could pull
divers from the future deep at this gold X
    of crossed thighs.

The moon would be carved soapstone, an Eskimo bird,
the stars little and prick. Like burrs. Like something
    plucked.
Or dropped, picked up. I am ready for this, blubber layer
    already shaped
into that peaked ovoid, dolphin or leaf.
My boy's jacket unzipped, I tell you the winds
    I'd run in
in my Arctic childhood (Manhattan).

Having been your teacher and probably not
    for the last time, I lecture
say I am cold not are you cold.

June

You can't hang a heavy mirror
on thin wire. "Don't buy a wire cutter,"
the man at the hardware store leers and mimes
pinching it with his fingers. Could I cut back
the hedge next door and would that
clear enough light for tomatoes? Or
"late mustard greens, late kale"
I hear an old gardener say, hear it
like a reprieve, I who miss deadlines,
spinach, broccoli, like qualifying exams
I can no longer choose to take. What a barbarian
I am at life, learning so late
these timings, the proper thicknesses. How
many tools do you need? What's the difference
between a wire cutter, a pruning
shears? Something that cuts through
something heavy.

First Harvest

Not the thunk of pumpkins, thicklidded,
    not zucchini almost
mammal in its nimbus of fur, not
    yet tomatoes
with a razor sliver of juice, not peppers
    each one a house
for the crinkly bitter proliferance
    of the seedcore
or the puckered, packed vision of sunflower, not yet
that which requires long summer,
    concrete

like a baker's oven, hot brick
and you almost go mad to get through it,
   not dig
and replete, fruit we put in
   year after year
tied in teepees, the antique pattern,
green on terra cotta; wish, toil, fulfillment.
But the gifts of the big old trees
   which sway

anyway, in rocky spring, glossy cherry, mulberry
   almost a problem, falling
white on the pavement, sweet as water.

Elizabeth Rees

Rockstar Poet

Her beauty bugs him
because, come on, he's busy.
But he laughs when his dog bites
her ankles, and he will have to
take her sooner or later.
Because he believes in signs

and she's got some set.
Even the dog pants for a lick.
But after he does her,
regret chills his teeth
gnats divebomb his bed.
And tomorrow he will try again

to write his way out, tomorrow
he will sing over her head.

Rita Mae Reese

Remembering Emily

While lying on the cold hood of her car
looking at a constellation I am unable to name
I wonder if death is lurking
like a battery thief in the next block.
I close my eyes and listen
to the hum of the distant highway
drowning out the savage stars.

The kitchen light leaves bright
squares on the grass. Inside,
she is laughing. My eyes closed,
I can see her petting a stray cat
on the church steps in the middle of the night
and I can see the distance
that has grown between us since.
I open my eyes and her laughter
is a constellation, old and blameless.

Adrienne Rich

Yom Kippur 1984

> I drew solitude over me, on the long shore.
> —Robinson Jeffers, "Prelude"

> For whoever does not afflict his soul throughout
> this day, shall be cut off from his people.
> —Leviticus 23:29

What is a Jew in solitude?
What would it mean not to feel lonely or afraid
far from your own or those you have called your own?
What is a woman in solitude: a queer woman or man?
In the empty street, on the empty beach, in the desert
what in this world as it is can solitude mean?

The glassy, concrete octagon suspended from the cliffs
with its electric gate, its perfected privacy
is not what I mean
the pick-up with a gun parked at a turn-out in Utah or the Golan
                              Heights
is not what I mean
the poet's tower facing the western ocean, acres of forest planted to
                       the east, the woman reading in the cabin, her
                       attack dog suddenly risen
is not what I mean

Three thousand miles from what I once called home
I open a book searching for some lines I remember
about flowers, something to bind me to this coast as lilacs in the
                    dooryard once
bound me back there—yes, lupines on a burnt mountainside,
something that bloomed and faded and was written down
in the poet's book, forever:
Opening the poet's book
I find the hatred in the poet's heart: . . . *the hateful-eyed*
and human-bodied are all about me: you that love multitude may have
                    them

Robinson Jeffers, multitude
is the blur flung by distinct forms against these landward valleys
and the farms that run down to the sea; the lupines
are multitude, and the torched poppies, the grey Pacific unrolling
                    its scrolls of surf,
and the separate persons, stooped
over sewing machines in denim dust, bent under the shattering
                    skies of harvest
who sleep by shifts in never-empty beds have their various dreams
Hands that pick, pack, steam, stitch, strip, stuff, shell, scrape,
                    scour, belong to a brain like no other
Must I argue the love of multitude in the blur or defend
a solitude of barbed-wire and searchlights, the survivalist's final
                    solution, have I a choice?

To wander far from your own or those you have called your own
to hear strangeness calling you from far away
and walk in that direction, long and far, not calculating risk
to go to meet the Stranger without fear or weapon, protection
                    nowhere on your mind?
(the Jew on the icy, rutted road on Christmas Eve prays for another
                    Jew
the woman in the ungainly twisting shadows of the street: *Make*
                    those be a woman's footsteps; as if she could believe in a
                    woman's god)

Find someone like yourself.   Find others.
Agree you will never desert each other.
Understand that any rift among you
means power to those who want to do you in.
Close to the center, safety; toward the edges, danger.
But I have a nightmare to tell: I am trying to say
that to be with my people is my dearest wish
but that I also love strangers
that I crave separateness
I hear myself stuttering these words
to my worst friends and my best enemies
who watch for my mistakes in grammar
my mistakes in love.
This is the day of atonement; but do my people forgive me?
If a cloud knew loneliness and fear, I would be that cloud.

To love the Stranger, to love solitude—am I writing merely about
                    privilege
about drifting from the center, drawn to edges,
a privilege we can't afford in the world that is,
who are hated as being of our kind: faggot kicked into the icy
                    river, woman dragged from her stalled car
into the mist-struck mountains, used and hacked to death
young scholar shot at the university gates on a summer evening
                    walk, his prizes and studies nothing, nothing
                    availing his Blackness
Jew deluded that she's escaped the tribe, the laws of her exclusion,
                    the men too holy to touch her hand;   Jew who has
                    turned her back
on *midrash* and *mitzvah* (yet wears the *chai* on a thong between her
                    breasts) hiking alone
found with a swastika carved in her back at the foot of the cliffs
                    (did she die as queer or as Jew?)

Solitude, O taboo, endangered species
on the mist-struck spur of the mountain, I want a gun to defend
        you
In the desert, on the deserted street, I want what I can't have:
your elder sister, Justice, her great peasant's hand outspread
her eye, half-hooded, sharp and true
And I ask myself, have I thrown courage away?
have I traded off something I don't name?
To what extreme will I go to meet the extremist?
What will I do to defend my want or anyone's want to search for
        her spirit-vision
far from the protection of those she has called her own?
Will I find O solitude
your plumes, your breasts, your hair
against my face, as in childhood, your voice like the mockingbird's
singing *Yes, you are loved, why else this song?*
in the old places, anywhere?

What is a Jew in solitude?
What is a woman in solitude, a queer woman or man?
When the winter flood-tides wrench the tower from the rock,
        crumble the prophet's headland, and the farms slide
        into the sea
when leviathan is endangered and Jonah becomes revenger
when center and edges are crushed together, the extremities
        crushed together on which the world was founded
when our souls crash together, Arab and Jew, howling our
        loneliness within the tribes
when the refugee child and the exile's child re-open the blasted and
        forbidden city
when we who refuse to be women and men as women and men are
        chartered, tell our stories of solitude spent in
        multitude
in that world as it may be, newborn and haunted, what will
        solitude mean?

Mary Susannah Robbins

Eclipse of the Moon

The moon was in eclipse last night: the stars
and wheat stood in a group of everything
against the soft black air, and everything
half-waited, light. The copper edge of force

stood to its smoky shadow: the moon fought
dark, first unaware, then sickle-safe
in umber. What light shone its huge curves gave,
and the white stars haloed that group. We sought

to hold the faces of the far warm black
in this new hold of suns that still look on.
And, when the glowing partial speech was done,
light lifted. The full oval entered back

out of its joint breathing with our dark.
The grey mist slowly rose, forgetting, low,
and every star, remote in undertow,
asked of us, what new struggle hits the mark?

Jennifer Rose

The Suicide

How long did you wait
For Hercules or some other thug
To shovel you out of the grave,
Bring you back like Alcestis,
Restored and smug,
Hardly a breath missed,
Saved?
Waiting, what revenge did you plot
for your Admetus,
The man whose death you'd caught,
Playing his slave,
Agreeing madly to his careful loss?
How the earth bullied its fallow freight,
Packed mud into every hollow
Like a wound!—
Was a selfish husband
Worth all that dark weight
Or that much sorrow?
Nothing will make *him* wish
Back your life for his,
A life he borrowed, then clutched.
Nothing will make him substitute ground
For touch.
At first playing dead,
With the bed left unmade
For a better rest,
Then Hercules late,
You, breathless Alcestis,
How long did you wait?

Ellen A. Rosen

Out in the Cold

My seventh summer the Rosenbergs burned in Sing Sing Prison,
leaving behind two small furious sons. All June, my parents
argued the fate of Julius and Ethel behind closed doors.
Words flew heavy, like a sick old crow. The Cold War nipped
my ears, roosting in my home. I studied my *Webster's*
to crack the codes confounding me, especially the "blacklist"
that froze my uncle's brilliant stage designs out of every theatre
in America. Winter came, & I enrolled in a local Sunday school
to study Torah, Hebrew & all things Jewish. At dinner, when I
interwove tales of May Day with the threads of Joseph's wondrous coat,
my father fumed, "Just wait. Wait till Sunday." All week,
fear scared my sleep. I prayed my father's rage would melt
& wash away. Sunday, he picked me up late & had me wait in the cold
while he reviled my teacher, Evie Cohen. I stomped & chattered,
forgotten for nearly an hour, while inside the cozy red house,
my father's lunatic voice steamed every window in every room.
He never guessed, he never knew, that outside in the icy morning air,
I was raging too, red-hot.

Mariève Rugo

Pietà

What she holds is the unimaginable
husk of the universe—
his life, hers, the known world
slipping apart from the familiar,
its pulse
his absence.
The clock is a mockery
of living. Everything
is a mockery
of living—the light inching
that wall, the stones, the weeping
friends trapped in their distances,
the way she cannot feel
the wind in the branches.
Once, he was small
in the dappled garden,
playing at going in and out
of his kingdom, his voice
a gold thread of birdsong.
In the sunlight, she inhaled
his perfection.

She has become the empty
room of her past,
her mouth filled
with gravel,
her flesh impaled
on that instant

he left
his body in her arms.
And it will always be
March, 1991.
She will always stand
with her hand on his coffin
in the sweet wilting scent
of daffodils, her hand
on the wooden shell
for his small hollow bones,
on this cold without thaw.

Kate Rushin

In Answer to the Question:
Have You Ever Considered Suicide

Suicide?!?!
Gurl, is you crazy?
I'm scared I'm not gonna live long enough
as it is

I'm scared to death of high places
Fast cars
Rare diseases
Muggers
Drugs
Electricity
And folks who work roots

Now what would I look like
Jumpin offa somethin
I got everything to do
And I ain't got time for that

Let me tell you
If you ever hear me
Talkin bout killin my frail self
Come and get me
Sit with me until that spell passes
And if they ever
Find me layin up somewhere
Don't let them tell you it was suicide
Cause it wasn't

I'm scared of high places
Fast moving trucks
Muggers
Electricity
Drugs
Folks who work roots
And home-canned string beans

Now with all I got
To worry about
What would I look like
Killin myself

Looking for W.E.B.

The lady behind the desk
at the Great Barrington, Massachusetts
public library is disturbed.
There's no display for this native son.

We didn't intend to cause a ruckus with our
presence, our unruly hair.
We only want to use the women's room,
pay our respects to Dr. DuBois.
She wonders if we're from Simon's Rock
as if the answer could explain us.

The memorial park turns out to be
an overgrown field where the house once stood.
Where Van Der Zee set up his tripod
on the porch, after lunch, to catch a glimpse of
the spirit of the elegant clan on a wistful,
summer day of never-ending accomplishment.

We laugh that laugh,
picturing Alice Walker
calling "Zora! Are you out here?"
searching for Hurston, our genius of the South
trampling through weeds
in an abandoned graveyard in Florida.

William, where are you? We like to think
our scholar of the north rests well in Ghana.
We pull aside the branches,
settle for snapshots next to the plaque.

Off another road
we wander into Dr. Schweitzer's center.
We are confronted by
larger-than-life-sized photographs:
The great man ministering to Africans
in Africa.

Word Problems

If a train departs at 10:20 P.M.
traveling south and another train
departs at 10:10 P.M. headed north,
what time will it be when we finally
take haven in an indulgent bed
marooned in a multi-national hotel room
overlooking Central Park?

How many hours will it be before the edges
soften and we walk through the park, smile at
strangers we wrongly assume to be
New Yorkers, sit in overpriced cafes,
sip international coffee drinks and cognac,
regard male nude portraits executed by
Sigmund Freud's grandson hanging in the
Metropolitan Museum of Art? What time shall we
return to room service remote and bourgeois bed
the dubious privilege of somebody else compelled
to make it? The next morning, exposed in our 1970's
campus-style Afro-Am cultural nationalism,
we'll overtip the Third-World-Woman cleaning staff
then see each other off at Amtrak
just in time to make it back to our good jobs.

Yet, somewhere between the maxed-out credit cards,
mini-bar and starched linens, two grown colored women
inscribe a story. It's a story some brother with an agenda
declared couldn't exist due to inauthenticity. Some sister with
self-induced amnesia pretended she couldn't read between the lines,
had no idea what we were talking about. Some white woman
insisted the story was interchangeable with hers
and some white man reported it was not in evidence;
we'd never crossed his mind.

We are the last generation
raised by 19th-century women, the link between
our great-grandmothers in bondage and our
daughters in cyberspace. No wonder
we're standing here wondering; inhabitants of a land
everybody wants to occupy, but nobody wants to imagine.
As our daughters and sons set out on the
MTV artificial intelligence information superhighway
we haunt the crossroads. We're on the watch to pass them
a few books, a few photos, a few stories, a few words;
a broach, a piece of cloth, a song, a prayer,
a pressed flower; a feather, a shell and a bone.
We maintain that the elite have nothing going for them
except money, technology, and all, all the while we fake
faith, hedge our bets: *Got to learn those computers.*
You'll go to that private school if I have my say.
We just can't risk stranding our children in that
so-called underclass we used to call home.
But like I said, there's nothing disembodied,
not what I'm talking about. Sign your name.
Turn off that television.
This ain't one of those nihilistic scenes lit by the despairing
blue light of the tube.
Find ourselves? Lose ourselves?
I don't claim to know the difference.
There's nothing to lose I haven't lost more times
than I thought possible. I won't hesitate or wait.
If we're lucky we'll get a corner room high enough to
catch a glimpse of the moon to remind us of other shores.
Put on some Nina or Coltrane,
Find Abby Lincoln on the FM stereo.

Incense, candle flame, papaya and cowry shell
mark the boundaries.
This body is home.
Look here.
This is the lush life
only for a minute.

Your train is traveling
south at 73 miles per hour.
Mine is headed north doing 68.
How long will it take us to arrive at
our separate definitions?
What time shall we begin, for real?
What time can we call it home?

Sonia Sanchez

Part Four: Rebirth

When i stepped off the plane i knew i was home.
had been here before. had been away
roaming the cold climate of my mind where
winter and summer hold the same temperature
of need.

and i held up my hands. face. cut by the northern
winds and my blood oozed forth kissed the place
of my birth and the sun and sea gathered round
my offering and we were one as night is surely day
when you truly understand the need one has for the
other.

a green smell rigid as morning
stretched like a young maiden 'cross the land
and i tasting a new geography took off my shoes
let my feet grow in the green dance of growth
and the dance was new and my thighs
burning like chords
left a trail for others to follow when
they returned home as all must surely do to make
past future tense.

the faces smiling at me, the sun drenched faces
like soft leather. they knew that i finally knew
and our eyes met. promised meetings. no words
were spoken for the speech of recognition had been
spoken and the constant movement to your place
of birth where the warm/blue/green seas cradle
your blackness.

the ritual beat of the sun and sea
made my body smile.

creases of laughter covered me
when i saw the sea. & the sea was shocked
by the roar of my laughter coming from my
bowels like some giant wave.
my pores sweated, expelled all past rhythms
brought the chants of one made tall
by the wisdom of suns.

i grew as i rowed out from boulevards
balancing my veins on sails
i grew as the clouds moving 'gainst chills
tilted my flesh till it flakes.
and i sang
              arch me softly
              O summery winds, i am
              strict as the sun.
                  rock me O pulse
              i knock all over.
              sing. sing. sing. you
              sister waves. i shall paint
              his silence with seeds.

i remembered the first time i made love
in a room on seventh avenue
on a street of forgotten tribal life
and as the sea entered my pores and
made me stretch and open to be filled
i remember a nite we stretched our
bodies and poured our juices into each other.
it was summer and you called me little one
for my body filled only a small part
of your need.

some faces gathered at the shore.
called out warnings as i walked further
from the land. some faces screamed
no one can grow as tall as the sea. but
i continued to grow and the sea and i greeted
each other with laughter.
each day she measured my growth and said one day

you'll be taller than i.
i cannot remember the color of day
when i had to bend to be caressed by her touch.

whatever is truth becomes known. nine
months passed touching a bottomless sea.
nine months i wandered amid waves
that washed away thirty years of denial.
nine months without stains

nine months passed and my body
heavy with the knowledge of gods
turned landward. came to rest.
wherefore a woman has many fathers,
i keep dreaming of my birth
of two hands moving against chills
tilting the flesh till it flaked.
i became mother of sun. moon. star children.
and the hour of after birth when i turned
into my breath you came and i proclaimed
you without sound.
you. you. Black Man. standing straight
as a sentry. staring in monotony.
Look. a savior moves in these breasts,
i who have waltzed the sea hear my
seed running toward your seasons.
you. you. Black redeemer star.
sweeten your points.
i need old silver for my veins.

Cheryl Savageau

Heart

i. When Grampa dies
   the tiny dancer in my chest
   climbs into my throat
   and kicks, kicks, kicks!
   I keep my mouth shut tight.

   In bed
   I hear her in my pillow.
   She has escaped!
   All night I chase her,
   now fast, now slow and tired,
   out of breath.

ii. In the cottage
    surrounded by rivers
    a woman is sweeping.
    A bird flies
    from window to window
    never staying in
    never staying out.

Betsy Sholl

You Figure It Out

Behind me the sunken face of a woman
is telling her kid sit down, shut up, don't
touch, I'm gonna kick your butt, while the kid
makes leftover filters speed up and brake
around the rim of an ashtray. I can't look.

Though the way she lifts her hand to him,
the way her mouth says *don't* even when it's
shut, is played out on my face in the bus
station window just as that silver hulk
pulls in and docks. I pop a pill

so I'm pale and luminous and can watch
without flinching because whatever they
can do to a body they can do to you.
Like last night some jerk getting kicked
till he had no face and I screamed *police*

because I was not hard enough: I wanted
to go home, only just then I couldn't
think where that was. Now the driver's flipping
his giant Rolodex on the bus forehead
through Providence, Hartford, New York. The woman's

confused, picks up her bashed in suitcase, bangs
the kid on each step till he starts to howl.
Next she'll be calling him *brat, trash,* gouging
a wad of used gum from his mouth. She'll jerk
him into the seat so his neck half snaps.

A whole childhood like that, and he'll end up
with me watching this battered bitch face
in the sky rise pocked and orange over
a little plaza of flat-roofed stores that'll
dry clean you in 24. Eyes sunken

from midnight's throaty deejay speed-rapping
desire. X-ray ears to pick up
the chipped rim of a woman's voice scratching
across her kid's back. I'd get totally
scrambled. My old lady would say, Don't let

me see you like this again, or Who the hell
do you think you are? Damned if I know.
But I can tease a street, or walk it brisk
if I want, alone, like I got someplace
to go. And now, most any city, I find

myself down at the docks watching water
break up whatever light happens to fall.
Whoever's out there moves in like every
slow song he ever heard is turning its
weird speed in his gut. Wants to touch something

Mama can't slap away. Wants to need me
till I can't resist. Pours his voice in my ear,
thick like he swallowed his tongue. To which I'd
reply—Only, hey—what is it a dog says,
when it throws back its head and doesn't stop?

Good News/Bad News

We're riding home from *Godspell,* which most people
cannot appreciate, my mother says, for lack of biblical
training. I hate to think of you, she continues, riding
these dirty trains—my mother, once again distinguishing
us from *them,* cultured from common. As if on cue,

the subway fizzles to a stop, and in the blackness
a woman starts to cry, her voice small as the First Aid siren

from childhood, slowly rising to an intolerable scream.
People stiffen in the dark. A few start to grope, maybe
toward her, maybe our wallets. She's Spanish,

so what I understand is the sheer decibels of panic,
that nightmare where you try to call a name, to cry out
what's happening, what's going on, but your tongue's too
thick, and when you open your mouth a whole sea rushes in.
Jesus, My God, will you shut up, somebody yells,

which unnerves my mother who slumps against me, claws
at my hand—a little street theater I hadn't intended,
her common element unhinging itself in a broken down train,
temperature rising, voices muttering *asshole* in the dark.
That's not how it seemed as we pulled out of Park Street,

rattling through the tunnel in our summer-thin clothes,
raggedy clowns and well-dressed betrayers, all the other
posible combinations—a jittery son planning to call home
collect, a hooker who's just emptied her purse for a friend,
a father who sees on the window glass the bloated face

of a gone child—all of us, I thought, underground,
and in a little while we'll surface, blinking in the light,
still Thursday's, late afternoon given back to us like a gift,
a few jet trails thinning in the sky. But this moment
changes all that, the way time stalls in our veins,

and we radiate a nervous heat, flapping newspapers
against the smothering air. It's quiet a minute,
then the woman starts up *O, O,* the rest in Spanish.
Someone blurts out *for Christ's sake,* and you can feel
people holding their breath, as if that could trip

the engines, flick the lights and fans back on,
answer what we're beginning to wonder—will we take
the usual neck-jerk curve and start to climb,
or does the woman we all want to shut up know
something she's trying to tell us, murmuring now,

deliberately, as if she's been through this
shuddering cave before and it's not what we think,
which makes my mother rasp as she breathes in the uneasy
stillness, big gulps of it, trying not to imagine
what other mouths it has already passed through.

The Postmaster's Children

Sometimes when they passed I'd touch the glass
and shiver, because they were just my size,
and even between the black bony silhouettes
of my favorite president taped on the class window,
I couldn't hide from their pudgy retarded faces,

blunt cut bangs, almond eyes, the way they waddled
after their squat mother, bumping together
when she stopped, then trudging again behind her
lugging groceries down the sandy shoulder
of the road past my school. Years later,

they're still living inside my face, rotting,
turning mournful. Their father was the postmaster.
He was also their mother's brother. I was sixteen
when the rotting inside his head stopped.
My uncle, the undertaker, laid him out

and I sneaked in to see how such convolutions end.
I was sixteen, but my heart raced like it was
still nine, straying down the creek road where
his horse stood at the fence, its dark profile
distinct as a president. One big brown moist eye,

then, a swing of its head, and I saw the other
all pus and flies. That came back to me
in my uncle's parlor, just the start of what I had
to remember—the road past that shack, the wooden
boardwalk of the old post office, its wanted posters

glaring at girlie poses on the opposite wall.
It's as if I had to enter the dead man's eye,
the same way I walked into his dark office the winter
I was nine, blinded by sunlight on snow, my pupils
slowly expanding, taking in more than anyone planned.

Who knows what the postmaster felt unzipping
the sealed letter of his pants, pulling out that news?
What was I supposed to do, standing there, one hand
full of Valentines, the other brimming with pennies—
no voice, no lids on my eyes, no feet that moved?

"You never seen it before," is all he said,
and then he showed me exactly what it was—me trying
to back toward the brightness outside, just as she
was coming in with the sticky pudge of their children
bunched up behind her, and all of us too stupid to move,

so we pressed together in the doorway, like something
he was shaping with his hand, me breathing fast like him,
breathing in wet wool, urine, the coppery chocolate
coating their tongues, their dull shockless eyes,
till something finally gave—the pennies clattered

and spun, the children bent to them, and I was outside
in the cold again, my eyes getting small, very small,
till none of this was left, just a shivery feeling
each time I saw them, and my red hearts which never
got sent, their flimsy envelopes scattered in the snow.

Beverly Jean Smith

The Saturday before Easter

I enter Ruth Flowers' School of Cosmetology
The echoes of scissors, dryers, and curlers tinkle
Against metal burners where each student buttoned
Inside a white uniform fastened hem to neck
Learns the ways of females and nails.

Seated, fingers work through each criss cross, parting
Threads of my plait softened from the weaving. Next,
I am lifted on top of two phone books. My neck rests
In the throat of the sink. Head tilted backwards
Water stings my scalp. One fluffy white hand towel
Is draped over my woolly hair for damp drying.
Sections are parted, twisted into ball-like thorns.
Under hooded heat I sit, wait.

Released, I am ushered to a black swivel chair
Coiled through the air. She dots my scalp with dabs of grease.
Chin to collar bone the iron tooth comb tugs through crinkles.
Singes my hair. I think of the hot clothes iron that once
Burned my brown wrist white and fold my ear tighter.
Strand upon strand the straightening continues angling
My head this way and that until it aches then numbs
From the weight of the downward pull.

A hum rises from my paralysis. Is it kin
To the white rabbit's thumping? Inside the glass cage,
Makeda's pet boa constrictor lassoed it,
Swallowed head first, one large smooth lump going down
Slow.

Ann Spanel

Pez Dorado

> The leafbud straggles forth
> toward the frigid light of the airshaft this is faith
> this pale extension of a day
> when looking up you know something is changing
> winter has turned though the wind is colder
> —Adrienne Rich

When I walk into the Pez Dorado I am always sad.
Hunger pulls me into this scoured poor Cuban-Chinese dive.
It rains inside, on the floors, on the counters, on the tables,
in the ashtrays, on the sugar-glasses.
No one is smoking here.

I spread my legs under the table. I am making love with something—
the silence, the cleanness, the bright fluorescent light.
The old Chinese man looks at me. He brings crushed mango/ice/milk
in a fluted plastic glass, cold thick unsweet.
I drink it carefully, a medicine for sadness. It makes me see

the pale vine that curls its arrowed tip at the end of winter
through your poem about Broadway.
Since you have moved from this block, I have mourned you
as though spring had aborted & left her leaf-thin foetuses
everywhere, scattered along the routes you took through the City.

Kathleen Spivack

The Scroll

Friend, how I have missed you,
setting pen to paper.
I have been on a long journey
and even now
I am travelling further away.
I have become
like the old man in the Chinese
scrolls, forever starting out again
in search of the horizon.

On the practical level
life has not worked out
too well:
turning my back
for an instant
it is as if love had never been,
nor my body
fallen away from its ecstasy
into a kind of bitterness
at rest.

Friend, I would like to begin again.
Today the wild roses
tell me perhaps that is
possible. The beach
sparkles with entrances.
I was hurt. I bled.
This would seem to have been appropriate.

But look, I am still walking around
the landscape; a hopeful animal,
a mendicant, a hobo:
parting the future, that mountainous
painting, with footsteps.

Sunday

It's Sunday:
in the suburbs of the heart they are
washing their cars.

She steams in the kitchen
along with the potatoes: dinner
takes ten minutes to consume.

And he gets up with the
children early: whoever
ain't got custody

can visit them today.
The flesh is prinked
and dressed up: the pastor

presses my hand as if he meant it.
The polar bear, behind bars,
gets up on his hind legs, sighing.

The Yearning throughout Life

When you wake at night
are there arms around you:
the swoop of a woman
pressing her rounded body
to yours, her hair?
Death is a tunnel

by which to enter light:
is it pain or
compassion that assists you?

The pillow case is creased,
no longer fresh. You turn
in the journey that is
no longer childhood.
But look,
the forest is still there,
the same darkness,
the same hopeless figures standing,
mother and father,
beside your bed.

And in the same familiar way,
you cannot speak to them.
Only this unutterable
white pain
as in a space capsule
surrounds you,
carrying you away
while at the same time
you appear to be not moving.

The high white hum of the room—
mother, father—oh see
what little ones they have become.
They, too, are dear
and innocent as terrified
trapped animals.

Now only the resolute circle
of someone lifting you up
and holding, near her
large courageous body, fiercely,
your enfolded sleep
can guide you
into daybreak.
She is the one
against whose warm side
you breathe softly,

in and out,
your small life-spark
like an eye,
a thought,
like a little joke.

Judith W. Steinbergh

Burial

It is Sunday, day of rest. My daughter is out, her pet rat
is scratching in his cage, rotund and senile, sedentary
and smelly, the darling of my daughter's life. I am paying
my bills: electric, water, news, throwing a little money at
my charge cards, trying to figure how the gas company got
control of my life; writing, tearing, licking, sealing,
when I reach the phone bill, the total, second only to
the national debt, the decimal point lost among all those
digits, numbers that repeat like rain, numbers my daughter
has gleaned from movie magazines, rockstar rags and friends
of friends, calls to Hollywood, Memphis, Staten Island,
San Diego, Juarez. My breathing is heavy,
my blood rises like the Charles in spring.
The door opens and bangs. My daughter is there
in her leather and makeup, my daughter, wearing black,
steps into trouble. I show her the bill. She doesn't know,
she says . . . her friends must have used our phone, she says,
she'll never touch it again. I am shaking, my hands have a
strange attraction to her neck, I am clutching them behind
me when—the rat dies—and indeed, the bloated rodent
is flat on its side, little claws curled permanently around
the air. I am a train that must brake for a cow. I am a plane
landing at an airport that is closed. My anger skids on the
asphalt. Funeral plans must be made. My daughter is wailing
like an ambulance, stroking her pet's cold snout. We
prepare a silken shroud, a cardboard coffin, we say our last
goodbyes and seal it in with packing tape so cats won't
scratch it out. I dig among old snow under the cherry,

a prime resting spot, I dig as deep as strife. We lay
the box among dark clods of dirt, sprinkle topsoil on, say
our prayers and psalms, poke in dried flowers and a cross
my daughter's borrowed from another site. I stare at her across
the yard's scar. If she hadn't loved that rat so hard,
I'd swear she planned its death. The phone bill waits,
still fresh, but I have buried the sharp claws of my anger,
its ugly tail. What is lost is something small and warm
I nurtured once, something I thought was my own.
My daughter goes inside to get the phone.

Religion

I am in the old *shul* between the railroad and the glass factory
and on the *bima* Mr. Goldberg is racing Mr. Horowitz through
the *ovenus.* They are both half dead. Their prayers live in them
like salt and when they *doven,* the prayers pour out. Uncle Ben
and Uncle Wolf have their own books, each a little different,
and their own tunes and their own wives whispering about their own
menopauses. *Leho adonai hagdulo,* the old rabbi sings bringing
the *torah* down the steps, down the aisle, slowly shuffling
toward me and Andra in the back row, where the slatted seats
are biting our bottoms. We hold our giggles in our throats with our
palms, he's here and we kiss our fingertips and touch the *torah*
and he's gone up the aisle and the step. The prayers
resume as a train screams by, drowning out all Judaism. Mr. Goldberg
doesn't flinch, his chants are soundless. It is a long one, we
count the cars by their clicks and picture oranges and trucks
stacked up and slats with cows between and rolls of glinting steel,
our giggles free now like doves in the sooty brick sanctuary until
the last car, the eighty-seventh, when the chanting emerges like
entrails from a train. Tomorrow we will kiss Billy in the base-
ment after Sunday school if the New York Express doesn't shake us
loose. These were the years I knew the motions but not the words,
a religion tied up with the B & O, a sacred scroll connected to
Billy Felder's lips, the old men reliable and insistent as the
roar that shook our *shul.*

Give Peace a Chance

I had to get an operation to get some peace. I didn't
actually go so far as to invent the symptoms (although
this is not out of the question), but I went leaping
into that hospital as if it were a plane ticket to the
islands, away from my kids and cooking and cleaning and
teaching and four classes a day. I took my most important
shells and stones and beads. My nurse Bessie winked
away a lot of rules like no sticking photos on the walls
and my nurse Lenora busied herself elsewhere while my man
lounged on my bed till real late that first night. Even
after the morphine and pentothal, teams of masked bandits
after my treasures, and lovely silk stitches, I lay afloat
on sunlight in my room again, at peace for the first time
in a decade, sipping ice water down a parched throat,
letting calm fill tip my knuckles and knees, my elbows,
the long curved fibula and the dark explored cavities
of my body. No way was I going home. I had to faint
in the lav to convince the staff to let me stay. The
daffodils opened their mouths gently and friends pushed
pastels like chips of sky and lips over rough paper.
I was thin and green as a leaf on a river. Oh give me
peace once in a long while.

Mary Louise Sullivan

Unearth

Something is always vanishing
and now it seems there is less

air to breathe. In the dimness
of night she says the word "Edinburgh."
She means "Edinburgh" as if she were
in an airplane holding her ears
to stop the sucking there. History
says she is flying somewhere,
but when she turns to reply
she is only leaning into the ruin

of sunlight, only shifting the weight
of memory. When he took her hand
the first time and they stopped talking
beneath the junipers in the early morning,

that is what she remembers best. Because
history has no mouth to protest the morning
and no one is singing of its new sun, she unearths
sounds like "Edinburgh" as she listens
for the sound of the sea:

She is trying to be polite,
but she misses him so much.

Wedding Song

Where the bridesmaid waits in the vestibule,
the walls shine of gold leaf and it smells
of oil. She is listening to the song that has
begun to come slowly down from above, the song
that seems to be the song that everyone has put
their trust into. Someone is playing the guitar
so carefully, its sound unseals the air. The song

Is everything, it cannot wait. But it's the absence
of the song that almost haplessly finds its way
to the ones waiting. In the absence of the song
we begin to unlearn what we have come to trust;

It makes us nearly crazy with wanting, with what
the song doesn't say. The child, who entering
the church, sees only the bright Christ hanging
at the altar, asks her mother, Why does he exist?
to which she answers, So we can remember
who we want to be; and when the child keeps
tugging on her mother's sleeve to ask again,
she signals, Shhh—for the music is playing. There
are so many people in here, it takes the girl's

Breath away. In the back pews of the church,
a young woman turns from her lover: she is afraid
of the song, which now that it has begun, must end.
It is the water rhythm of the guitar rolling away
like footsteps leaving a porch in the night, the steps,
the sand, the horseshoe crab, leaving, tucking beneath
the rib cage like a scar. If she could let the song
go, she could begin to unlearn the end, she could
begin. When she turns back to her lover, she knows

She will leave him. If he could stop and hear
the song, the father of the bride might be able
to recall something about his own wedding,
or know if it were a moment, or an hour, or a day
when he stopped loving his wife and she him.
But, it doesn't matter: in the basement of the church
where the music slips in like old, quiet whispering,
the father cannot leave the bathroom. All he can see

Is the white of the toilet bowl around him. Though
it is easiest to see his fear in the winter, when,
like the air, it is cold and blue and seems to control
the world, now it is August. If he could only listen;
for anyone can see that outdoors the dogwoods, the
magnolias and lilacs have blossomed. The song
cannot wait any longer. The song goes like this.

Kate Taylor

Wheel Building

The shiny roundness of the rim
rests in my lap,
hub held in the center

with the tingle, jingle of loose spokes
dropping into place, dangling
in the unsupported hub.

Then placing the first spoke,
freewheel side down, offsets to the left.
The pattern begins:

every fourth hole, thread the nipple loosely,
flip the wheel, repeat, flip back
and repeat again, Pleasing geometry.

Triple cross? Double cross.
The pattern taking shape.
The rim now holds the hub.

Loose at first, spokes flex
in and out like breath.
Pulling up

brings the wheel closer to strength.
Two passes, half turn, keep it consistent;
start at the valve hole, don't lose track.

Still loose, check round,
tighten here, and here.
Pull again, quarter turn,

check true, check round, check tension.
It's looking good. Spokes take up the slack.
The calipers are steady on the rim.

The new wheel balances,
spokes taut, as the hub
shines in the center.

Lee Varon

Pink magnolias, the punishment

The magnolia buds
grew like angels' hearts,
swollen pearls . . .
In spring
hundreds rose from the
tree in your grandmother's

yard, delicate tips
balancing the gauze
of green sky. A child,
you began to count
them and grew dizzy,

fell down in the grass.
At this moment you
had a beautiful
childhood, rolling down
the hill in a white

pinafore . . . You
remember, mornings,
running to lift your
pet rabbit from its
cage. Burying your face

in its belly you
felt its heart thump against
your cheek as you offered
carrots, wilted lettuce,
brown pellets from a

jade bowl. You try to
forget the spider
she planted   as large
as your face   as still
as the wire it clung to

in your rabbit's cage.
You try to see only
the magnolias as
if each vein were etched
in your hand. The

magnolias were your
way of not looking;
until she held your face
tightly in her two hands
and made you look   as

your rabbit froze, its
red eyes dilating
past death into a place
you never wanted to
see again and yet

you did see—how many
minutes did you stand
as your rabbit an inch
from you quivered at
the tip of each hair

and the spider like
black grass moved over
the rest of your life.

Cornelia Veenendaal

Sun-crossed

Before I ever saw this room
I knew it
as I know the September sun
at its brightest.

Her sleigh bed,
folded India shawl,
beyond the windows, evergreens
blue as estrangement.

Here is discipline
say the proportions.
Here is all you need
in life.

In a straight chair
at a small square table
Emily Dickinson
is writing.

Make me a picture of the sun—
So I can hang it in my room—

Her columnar self
a gnomon in the light;
now she crosses the seagrass mat
barefoot to the Spice Isles.

Rosmarie Waldrop

Excerpt from *Lawn of Excluded Middle*

It's a tall order that expects pain to crystallize into beauty. And we must close our eyes to conceive of heaven. The inside of the lid is fertile in images unprovoked by experience, or perhaps its pressure on the eyeball equals prayer, in the same way that inference is a transition toward assertion, even observing rites of dawn against a dark and empty background. I have read that female prisoners to be hanged must wear rubber pants and a dress sewn shut around the knees because uterus and ovaries spill with the shock down the shaft.

Lynne Weiss

Other Tongues

Lately she thinks
of exile. After dark
she studies a foreign language, shapes
her mouth to hold exotic sounds. In sleep
she dreams of lying
with men whose faces she can't see.

During the day she tells children
stories of brave immigrants.
She wants to say:

Those immigrants weren't brave
they were desperate like a woman
in a window
her hair and clothes on fire
throwing her child
into the arms of a person whose face
she cannot see
before she jumps herself.

And:
It wasn't the immigrants
who made our country
what it is. Don't blame them.
She desires mystery, secrets

wants to open cans
with indecipherable labels.
She doesn't want to know
what food she will eat
until it is on her tongue.

She is tired of seeing slick American
cars full of oil from another land.
She wants to be at home
in a strange country
where the cars are all foreign
and the language
men whisper when they enter
her is one of which she has no memories.

Jeanne Wells

July Thirteenth

Even opening my eyes
is an exercise in gravity today

I go through the list while lying in
bed: angry, lonely, sorry, afraid.

The thickness of sheets tangling
my arms and legs turns me into

a dwarf in my own life. The cure is
coffee, maybe walking—anything to smash the density.

What I really need, I decide, is to
dream of my dead mother, my own flesh

crossing the room, arms open, her hands gathering
yarrow and bones, the scat of my life. Efficient,

her ghost makes definition of it all;
I remember her form at the kitchen mirror

her red winter coat and thick wool scarf, she is
putting on lipstick, turning to go.

Ruth Whitman

Hearing a Mozart Duo at 36,000 Feet

> . . . the intimate, untranslatable news
> that music tells us . . .
> —Jorge Luis Borges

This cosmic
conversation
is holding
my body up.

Riding above
the weather
the viola
reminds me

there's no weather
up here,
no whale-streaked
ocean, no

bearded heads
of wheat, only
a round vacuum
of night

with the sun
always somewhere
else. The mind
misreads itself,

flesh continues
its descent
towards dust,
and I am part

of the viola's
theme: trapped
in a disparity
of aluminum and air,

but sustained
by the violin's
tender
counterpoint:

buoyancy,
despair.

Lee Whitman-Raymond

Quickening

just a hunch, really
a handful of pebbles
        shivers open the pond
one thrush fluting at first light
a lot of little leaves
        rustling

Louise Grassi Whitney

Beautiful Eyes

A thirty-year-old man in a highly-thought-of group home (regarded as humane) was distinguished by his penchant for collecting Grateful Dead t-shirts, given to him by the staff and his parents. A visitor offering him his first chance to use facilitated communication asked him, in making conversation, if he really liked collecting the t-shirts. His typed response was, "No, but the staff like them." Asked what he would prefer to receive he typed, "An education." This man was asked if we could repeat his story. He typed "yes if you tell them I have beautiful eyes."

Carla Willard

To the Station

Little socks fly, pink,
ragged white—
lace cuff turned up, now
over the frozen yard, now the sidewalk.
Bare legs running, mother's screams
split above in two
rooms, and her girl believing,
the invisible, wings,
took two flights
of stairs in six,
bounds into
dawn breaking as
red, the eye
shot through with the shape
of the mess, feet spinning, two-
pointed pinwheel on the cracked
cement, hair swept into
the senseless
air, and under
cotton panties working
into the arch, pulled,
like a tendon.

She never felt the glass.
Even when the red seeped
on the station floor, she slid
over this stain, and that stain.
She sang out, sudden, shrill
ruin, the not of her words, and across
the room, the policemen turned
heavy, tipsy, the desk sergeant slow-
reaching for a pen, as if there were
water, all under
water, the crooked
light, the crooked star.

Jeanette I. Winthrop

The Couple Having Breakfast in the Deli

They sit next to each other on the rose plastic bench,
their gray hair sometimes touching.
They speak so softly
no one can hear their breathing.
When the toasted muffins arrive, he spreads the butter
into every corner, and then the jam,
offering her the first half.
She accepts, breaks the muffin into small
pieces, barely chewing.

How alike they are as they eat;
their bones move inside their loose skin,
their true selves slowly shrinking.
Someday nothing will be left.
He leans over and brushes a crumb from her sleeve.
Her hands try and fail
and so he slips each button through each hole
and pushes with thin fingers
the sweater off her narrow shoulders.
I watch from across the room,
find it hard not to yell aloud,
me, me, who will love me like that?

S. L. Wisenberg

Casino

I've forgotten everything but the Good Two
and Good Ten. They were people the same way
my fingers had personalities:
kingly thumb, pointer old maid, suave bachelor
middle, flirtatious ring finger,
sly baby. Like the Good Two,
small and dark and coveted. Curled to herself.
Waiting, knowing she was wanted all game long.

The Good Ten was a faraway Prince Charming:
precision red diamonds, double breasted. A West Pointer
who dated the babysitter across the street.

But you turned to solitaire. Was it before the boy
in the silver-studded jacket swept me
from the house onto his motorcycle, before I
stuffed my diary full of dreams of flesh-and-blood princes,
before I felt the magic of the Good Two leave me, days at a time?

Did you one day look down,
and see your young partner
who had your brown eyes and square hands
and in a flash know the eyes
could never be level with yours,
the hands never know all of you,
and then did you deal two hands
for the last time?

Francine Witte

Prom

The one you shake your head over
those mornings you stare naked
into a cold mirror
and wonder what you ever had
that held up a strapless gown.

It's the one you went to dateless,
ashamed. That night, your mother pinned you
with an embarrassed corsage, wished you

a wonderful time. But you walked
into the high school gym like
a vaudeville clown who goes stagestruck

and knows the crowd smells blood.
You stand at the door till a horn-rimmed
boy from bio lab greets you, asks
you to dance. The Mello-Tones sway

the room like a mind half made up.
He asks you again and you're too shy
to say no. Near you, couples press close.

He squeezes your waist, asks
if you "do it."
This is a kid you wouldn't cut

frogs with. When he asks you again,
the music stops. The room flinches
with light. He says he's got a cousin
who'll let you spend the night.
You are on the verge of speech.

When You Call Again

I want your body
to stop short as you reach
for the phone.
I want you
to wonder if it's really
such a good idea.
I want you to do it anyway.

When you call again
I want to be thinking
of phrases like
"I need some space"
and "she meant nothing
to me." I want to remember
I last heard them from you.

When you call again
I want to be staring
into a mirror, seeing myself,
maybe for the first time-
I want my hands to be busy
holding my hair in different styles.
I want to be trying on clothes.

When you call again
I want the phone to ring
so loud and so often
that the neighbors come
to knock, check that I'm not
dead, have them relieved
to find me sitting on the patio,
flipping through a book,
biting into a peach.

But most of all,
when you call again
I want not
to answer the phone.

Nancy Means Wright

Acrophobia

Fay's reading Virginia Woolf: how a
woman ought to have five hundred pounds
and a room of her own. Well, Fay's got
the room all right—ten flights up and over-
looking the condo next door—if you
lean out the bathroom window you can see a
slice of the sky according to the landlord
and sometimes the handle on the Big

Dipper. . . . Only Fay's got acrophobia. Open
the window and her knees quake, stomach
wheezes, blood leaks into her toes and Fay
collapses in a bang of bones.
                              Still Woolf
holds something for Fay: how many over-fifties
walk out on their husbands with only the coat
on their backs, rocks in their pockets—where's
the five hundred pounds now? So Fay sticks

up stars on the bathroom ceiling, half moon
over the toilet while she pees, *To the
Lighthouse* next to the bottle of Zinfandel
and the mink oil bath beads by the four-
legged tub; red Gloxinia in the window and
snaps of the grand-kids in each cracked
pane. When Fay gets a yen for the Big

Dipper she's only to look at those faces—
one's got the sidesaddle grin Fay had
back in grade school the time she told the
lie about Uncle Don who read the comics
on the radio being her Uncle Don on the
dole in Tent City: for a whole week
until they found out Fay was the big

kid in town, Fay was her own star in the
tub, pie on the sly, moon in the toilet, Big
Dipper, Fay was a Room of her Own.

Robyn Zappala

Hope

She has a way of standing as if a belt of weights
has just been lifted from her hips. Tossing back
a drink, she feels her mother behind her, a mean ghost
crooning in the backroom. Three more and she'll
be saying anything that sounds like she's thought it
before. Hey, you want to whisper, hey.
The black man playing guitar smiles because he knows
he's losing. I'm gonna love you like you never
been loved before. Her hands are so heavy you feel them
on you minutes after she's taken them away. What she's
telling you now is anyone's guess, but you carry the tug
of her pain like a small anchor in your groin. Leaving,
you float like night air into the quiet, her lips
against your face under a streetlight, the brush
of a skiff over dark water.

One Year Later

I have moved to the house by the sea
I keep dreaming of. Each day the ocean
reaches to the stone foundation

and if I stand at the kitchen window
I am surrounded by water
and can feel the floor shift beneath me

buoyant and flexible in the tide.
What I used to fear has become routine for me—
uncalibrated time, bearded men

who patrol the beach like fathers shouting
obscenities, how quickly dark comes.
By the glow of one lamp I arrange the shells

I've found trapped beneath the baseboards
according to shades of copper; the largest one, unbroken,
resembles most your powdery skin.

One dirty gull pecks at the backyard feeder
though I keep it empty to discourage her.
You never come to visit.

I wait for the sun to sleep, comfortable only
in its glare that erases the image
of a woman turning away

from something that frightens her,
something small enough to cradle in her hand
but, for some reason, she has grown afraid of,

so warm and holy in her palm.

Rosamond Zimmermann

Anemia

to my daughter

On the eve of your transfusion
I'm thinking about ordering seeds
which I will force before spring,
about the garden of tomatoes
early girls which will rise
from the now frozen beds I built last fall.
I'm thinking I made a mistake in placing
them so squarely in a row on the lawn,
how, come spring, I will turn them so
they will radiate out beyond
the curve of the stone wall I labored
to create. I'm thinking about the necessity of thinking
ahead if we're to survive,
about having more children.

You say, *Now.* You say,
No. There will be no garden.
You draw my blood, you take
me with you, draining the blue.
There will be no garden.
You whiten, change
to cloud in my eyes erased
—absolutely colorless.

Marilyn Zuckerman

In Every Pot and Closet

It's dangerous to be too comfortable.
The old man knew that.
When my father's father,
the one my mother
called *the wandering Jew,*
died at ninety-six
he still had all his marbles.
Every couple of years,
he pulled up stakes,
renewed rage,
sharpened paranoia,
looked in every pot and closet for decadence.
Seeking the millenium, he made himself a nuisance.

Grandfather,
though I would fling those old testaments
out into deepest space,
along with your armlets
and the sign that lay upon your forehead
every morning, thanking Jehovah
you are not a woman—
Still, old wanderer,
how I follow in your footsteps.

Martha Zweig

Fleshpot

He trekked his body.
He pitched camp at the
bloodstream & fished there for
fishes: how they
seized on & flipped
up to his fondness,
beauties, crosshatched
all lights, colored
marmalade, tourmaline.

He's hungry. He cooks.
The thick of things
kicks in. Minutely he
pinches this &
that into the roil &
seethe to flavor the
chaos, chaos: how
much of sweet reason, rough
approximate love?

He will bed him in
luxury, vessels &
lungs. He will sleep
under his breath & dream
by leaps & bounds.
His scavengers
will tug details of
praise from the heap he will
leave them to overrun.

Acknowledgments

Grateful acknowledgment is extended to the following for permission to include their poems in this anthology:

Kathleen Aguero: "Looking for Another Version" and "Working Mother" reprinted by permission of the author.

Nadya Aisenberg: "The Woman in the Moon" reprinted by permission of the author.

Alma Stacey Allen: "Road Trip" reprinted by permission of the author.

Carol Arber: "Sketching in Barnstable" reprinted by permission of the author.

Rebecca Baggett: "Barely Eight" reprinted by permission of the author.

Carol Baker: "Your Going" reprinted by permission of the author.

Jane Barnes: "Passion at Forty" reprinted by permission of the author.

Ellen Bass: "All the Trees" reprinted by permission of the author.

Robin Becker: "Incarnate," "The Subject of Our Lives," and "Selective Memory" from *Giacometti's Dog* by Robin Becker. © 1990 by Robin Becker. Reprinted by permission of the University of Pittsburgh Press.

T Begley: "Sappho's Gymnasium" from *Prayerfields* by T Begley and Olga Broumas. © 1994 by Olga Broumas and T Begley. Reprinted by permission of the authors.

Sally Bellerose: "Bye Bye Barbara" reprinted by permission of the author.

Deborah Boe: "Jigsaw Puzzle" reprinted by permission of the author.

Marguerite Guzman Bouvard: "Landscape" reprinted by permission of the author.

Olga Broumas: "Sappho's Gymnasium" from *Prayerfields* by T Begley and Olga Broumas. © 1994 by Olga Broumas and T Begley. Reprinted by permission of the authors.

Polly Brown: "This Is for Megan" reprinted by permission of the author.

Ruth Buchman: "Short Story" reprinted by permission of the author.

Claudia Buckholts: "Old Woman Reclining" reprinted by permission of the author.

Leslie Burgess: "The Prostitute's Notebook" reprinted by permission of the author.

Carli Carrara: "On Weekends" reprinted by permission of the author.

Naomi Feigelson Chase: "He Comes to Lie Down," "Plenty," and "My Mother, Listening to Flowers" reprinted by permission of the author.

Eli Clare: "Learning to Speak" and "This Familiarity" reprinted by permission of the author.

Lynne Cohen: "Body Doubled" reprinted by permission of the author.

Martha Collins: "Re:composition" reprinted by permission of the author.

Elizabeth Crowell: "Portraits of the Ladies" reprinted by permission of the author.

Cortney Davis: "What Man Might Kill" from *Details of Flesh* by Cortney Davis. © 1997 by Cortney Davis. Reprinted by permission of the author.

Carol Dine: Excerpts from "Fugue" reprinted by permission of the author.

Rita Dove: "Sonnet in Primary Colors" from *Sojourner: The Women's Forum* 14:8 (April 1989). Reprinted in *Mother Love* by Rita Dove. © 1995 by Rita Dove. Published by W. W. Norton and Company, Inc. Reprinted by permission of the author. All rights reserved.

Frances Driscoll: "Real Life" from *The Rape Poems* by Frances Driscoll. © 1997 by Frances Driscoll. Published by Pleasureboat Studios. Reprinted by permission of the author.

Nancy Esposito: "Doing Good" reprinted by permission of the author.

Liz Fenton: "Places" reprinted by permission of the author.

Caroline Finkelstein: "Persephone's Notes," "Afterthought," and "Casus Belli" reprinted by permission of the author.

Janice Finney: "Lightning and Thunder" reprinted by permission of the author.

Sarah Fox: "Interruption" reprinted by permission of the author.

Kathleen Fraser: "One is whole. One is not" reprinted by permission of the author.

Erica Funkhouser: "Lillies" from *Sure Shot and Other Poems* by Erica Funkhouser. © 1992 by Erica Funkhouser. Published by Houghton Mifflin and Co. Reprinted by permission of the author.

Kinereth Gensler: "Bowl with Pine Cones" reprinted by permission of the author.

Celia Gilbert: "Questions about the Sphinx" reprinted by permission of the author.

Nikki Giovanni: "Forced Retirement" and "Crutches" reprinted by permission of
the author.

Beckian Fritz Goldberg: "Eros in His Striped Shirt," "My Husband's Bride," "Say,"
and "Hound and Leper" reprinted by permission of the author.

Stephanie Goldstein: "At Night" reprinted by permission of the author.

Miriam Goodman: "Poems from a Country House" reprinted by permission of the
author.

Valerie Graham: "You Know" reprinted by permission of the author.

Anne Haines: "Catching the Scent" reprinted by permission of the author.

Vanessa Haley: "Gangrene" and "Miss Gee Meets W. H. Auden in Heaven" reprint-
ed by permission of the author.

Marie Harris: "Trial Separation" reprinted by permission of the author.

Lola Haskins: "Message" and "The Shoes" reprinted by permission of the author.

Lyn Hejinian: Excerpts from *Sight* (Edge Books, 1999) by Lyn Hejinian and Leslie
Scalpino. © 1999 by Lyn Hejinian and Leslie Scalapino. Reprinted by permis-
sion of the authors.

Jan Heller Levi: "Tuscarora" reprinted by permission of the author.

Fanny Howe: "Crossing Out" reprinted by permission of the author.

Lynne Hugo: "Small Power" reprinted by permission of the author.

Julie Kalendek: "No part of the hand was hungry" reprinted by permission of the
author.

Kathryn Kirkpatrick: "Class" reprinted by permission of the author.

Stephanie Koufman: "Violins tickling" reprinted by permission of the author.

Ruth Lepson: "October 7, 1994" and "They were gliding" reprinted by permission of
the author.

Denise Levertov: "Arctic Spring" from *Evening Train* by Denise Levertov. © 1992 by
Denise Levertov. Reprinted by permission of New Directions Publishing Corp.

Lyn Lifshin: "The Child We Won't Have Is Crowding Us in the Front" and "Curling
on the Bottom of My Mother's Bed" reprinted by permission of the author.

Margo Lockwood: "Bookshop in Winter" reprinted by permission of the author.

Audre Lorde: "Dahomey" from *Collected Poems* by Audre Lorde. © 1978 by Audre Lorde. Reprinted by permission of W. W. Norton and Company, Inc.

Ruth Maassen: "Confessions of a Pisciphobe" reprinted by permission of the author.

Michelle M. Maihiot: "Playing Fields" reprinted by permission of the author.

Jennifer Markell: "The Veterinary Student" reprinted by permission of the author.

Suzanne Matson: "The Beach" and "Worry" reprinted by permission of the author.

Linda McCarriston: "Kitchen Terrarium" reprinted by permission of the author.

Helena Minton: "Day Surgery Pre-op" and "Building the Compost" reprinted by permission of the author.

Honor Moore: "To Janet, on *Galileo*," from *Memoir* by Honor Moore, and "Blues" reprinted by permission of the author.

Rosario Morales: "Old" from *Getting Home Alive* by Aurora Levins Morales and Rosario Morales. © 1986 by Rosario Morales. Published by Firebrand Books. Reprinted by permission of the author.

Robin Morgan: "Damn You, Lady" © 1986 by Robin Morgan. Reprinted by permission of the author from *Upstairs in the Garden: Poems Selected and New* by Robin Morgan (W. W. Norton, 1990).

Kate Mullen: "Thin-legged Lover" reprinted by permission of the author.

Nina Nyhart: "Vow," "The Shoes," and "Playing the Part" reprinted by permission of the author.

Dzvinia Orlowsky: "To Our Cosmeticians" from *A Handful of Bees* by Dzvinia Orlowsky. © 1994 by Dzvinia Orlowsky. Published by Carnegie Mellon University Press. Reprinted by permission of the author.

Molly Peacock: "Dogged Persistence" and "The Raptor" from *Original Love* by Molly Peacock. © 1995 by Molly Peacock. Reprinted by permission of the author and W. W. Norton and Company, Inc.

Joyce Peseroff: "After the Argument" reprinted by permission of the author.

Carol Potter: "White Hotel" and "In the Upstairs Window" reprinted by permission of the author.

Martha Ramsey: "Moving Out" from *Blood Stories* by Martha Ramsey. © 1996 by Martha Ramsey. Published by the Cleveland State University Poetry Series. Reprinted by permission of the author.

Jane Ransom: "This Is Just a Fairy Tale" reprinted by permission of the author.

Mary Kathleen Rayburn: "A Hurdler Explains Her Reasons" reprinted by permission of the author.

Monica Raymond: "Crossing the River," "June," and "First Harvest" reprinted by permission of the author.

Elizabeth Rees: "Rockstar Poet" reprinted by permission of the author.

Rita Mae Reese: "Remembering Emily" reprinted by permission of the author.

Adrienne Rich: "Yom Kippur 1984" from *Your Native Land, Your Life: Poems by Adrienne Rich.* © 1986 by Adrienne Rich. Reprinted by permission of the author and W. W. Norton and Company, Inc.

Mary Susannah Robbins: "Eclipse of the Moon" reprinted by permission of the author.

Jennifer Rose: "The Suicide" reprinted by permission of the author.

Ellen A. Rosen: "Out in the Cold" reprinted by permission of the author.

Mariève Rugo: "Pietà" reprinted by permission of the author.

Kate Rushin: "In Answer to the Question: Have You Ever Considered Suicide," "Looking for W.E.B.," and "Word Problems" reprinted by permission of the author.

Sonia Sanchez: "Rebirth" from *Blues Book for Blue Black Magical Woman* by Sonia Sanchez. © 1974. Published by Broadside Press. Reprinted by permission of the author.

Cheryl Savageau: "Heart" reprinted by permission of the author.

Leslie Scalapino: Excerpts from *Sight* by Lyn Hejinian and Leslie Scalapino. © 1999 by Lyn Hejinian and Leslie Scalapino. Reprinted by permission of the authors.

Betsy Sholl: "You Figure It Out" from *The Red Line* by Betsy Sholl. © 1992 by the University of Pittsburgh Press. Reprinted by permission of the University of Pittsburgh Press. "Good News/Bad News" and "The Postmaster's Children" reprinted by permission of the author.

Beverly Jean Smith: "The Saturday before Easter" reprinted by permission of the author.

Ann Spanel: "Pez Dorado" reprinted by permission of the author.

Kathleen Spivack: "The Scroll," "Sunday," and "The Yearning throughout Life" reprinted by permission of the author.

Judith W. Steinbergh: "Burial," "Religion," and "Give Peace a Chance" from *A Living Anytime* by Judith W. Steinbergh. © 1988. Published by Talking Stone Press. Reprinted by permission of the author.

Mary Louise Sullivan: "Unearth" and "Wedding Song" reprinted by permission of the author.

Kate Taylor: "Wheel Building" reprinted by permission of the author.

Lee Varon: "Pink magnolias, the punishment" reprinted by permission of the author.

Cornelia Veenendaal: "Sun-crossed" reprinted by permission of the author.

Rosmarie Waldrop: Excerpt from *Lawn of Excluded Middle* by Rosmarie Waldrop. © 1993 by Rosmarie Waldrop. Published by Tender Buttons. Reprinted by permission of Tender Buttons.

Lynne Weiss: "Other Tongues" reprinted by permission of the author.

Jeanne Wells: "July Thirteenth" reprinted by permission of the author.

Ruth Whitman: "Hearing a Mozart Duo at 36,000 Feet" reprinted by permission of the author.

Lee Whitman-Raymond: "Quickening" reprinted by permission of the author.

Louise Grassi Whitney: "Beautiful Eyes" reprinted by permission of the author.

Carla Willard: "To the Station" reprinted by permission of the author.

Jeanette I. Winthrop: "The Couple Having Breakfast in the Deli" reprinted by permission of the author.

S. L. Wisenberg: "Casino" reprinted by permission of the author.

Francine Witte: "Prom" and "When You Call Again" reprinted by permission of the author.

Nancy Means Wright: "Acrophobia" reprinted by permission of the author.

Robyn Zappala: "Hope" and "One Year Later" reprinted by permission of the author.

Rosamond Zimmermann: "Anemia" reprinted by permission of the author.

Marilyn Zuckerman: "In Every Pot and Closet" reprinted by permission of the author.

Martha Zweig: "Fleshpot" from *What Kind* by Martha Zweig. © 2002 by Martha Zweig. Reprinted by permission of Wesleyan University Press. All rights reserved.

Contributors

Kathleen Aguero is an associate professor of English at Pine Manor College in Chestnut Hill, Massachusetts. She is the author of two volumes of poetry, *The Real Weather* (Hanging Loose Press, 1987) and *Thirsty Day* (Alice James Books, 1977), and coeditor of three collections of multicultural literature: *A Gift of Tongues* (1987), *An Ear to the Ground* (1989), and *Daily Fare* (1995), all published by the University of Georgia Press. Her manuscript "Daughter of Sycorax" has been a finalist in several contests.

Nadya Aisenberg wrote four books of nonfiction and five poetry collections, including *Leaving Eden* (Forest Books, 1995) and *Measures* (Salmon Publishing, 2001), which was published posthumously.

Alma Stacey Allen writes poetry and teaches the psychology of women at the Sage Colleges in Albany, New York.

Carol Arber worked for many years in a college library. She writes, paints, and makes collages.

Rebecca Baggett lives with her family in Athens, Georgia, where she works as an academic advisor in the Franklin College of Arts and Sciences at the University of Georgia. She is the author of *Still Life with Children* (1996) and *Rebecca Baggett: Greatest Hits 1981–2000* (2001), both from Pudding House Publications.

Carol Baker lives in western Massachusetts and works as a mental health counselor. She has an MFA from the University of Iowa and has published poems in *The Nation, Stand, Ploughshares,* the *Massachusetts Review,* and other journals. She hopes to use writing for healing and empowerment in working with trauma survivors.

Jane Barnes, a transplant from Boston after thirty years, lives in Manhattan, agenting a long epistolary novel. She is also wantonly writing a one-woman show and delving into the theater and writing lyrics. She teaches a novel-writing class through the Learning Annex in Manhattan and is a novel development coach. Her work has been published in *Ploughshares, River Styx,* and a dozen anthologies.

Ellen Bass teaches creative writing in Santa Cruz, California, and has her own Web site, <http://www.ellenbass.com>. Her most recent book of poetry is *Mules of Love* (BOA Editions, 2002). She is also the author of nonfiction books including *Free Your Mind* (HarperCollins, 1996) and *The Courage to Heal* (HarperCollins, 1993).

Robin Becker is a professor of English and women's studies at the Pennsylvania State University and serves as poetry editor for *The Women's Review of Books.* Her fifth book of poems is *The Horse Fair* (University of Pittsburgh Press, 2000). The Frick Art and Cultural Center in Pittsburgh, Pennsylvania, published *Venetian Blue,* a chapbook of poems about the visual arts, in 2002.

T Begley is a poet, teacher, and founder of an evolving workshop series that spans *Writing the Five Elements, By Heart,* and *Kind.* Her publications include *Sappho's Gymnasium* (Copper Canyon Press, 1994), collaborative poems with Olga Broumas, and *Open Papers* (Copper Canyon Press, 1995), translations with Olga Broumas of the selected essays of the Greek poet Odysseas Elytis. She is at work on "The Minds of Prayers: Acts for Poets" and "Diary of the Still."

Sally Bellerose received a fellowship in prose from the National Endowment for the Arts to finish "The GirlsClub," a novel for which she has recently found an agent. She is working on a second novel titled "Legs."

Deborah Boe is the recipient of a National Endowment for the Arts fellowship and two fellowships from the New Jersey State Council on the Arts. She is the author of *Mojave* (Hanging Loose Press, 1987), and her poems have appeared in *Poetry, Poetry Northwest, Ohio Review,* and other magazines.

Marguerite Guzman Bouvard is a resident scholar with the Women's Studies Research Center at Brandeis University. She is the author of four books of poetry and several books of nonfiction.

Olga Broumas is the author of *Rave: Poems 1975–1999* (Consortium Book Sales and Distributors, 1999), *Perpetua* (Copper Canyon Press, 1989),

Pastoral Jazz (Copper Canyon Press, 1999), *Ithaca—Little Summer in Winter* (Radiolarian Press, 1996), and many other books.

Polly Brown shares her poetry work with the Boston-area collaborative Every Other Thursday and teaches at Touchstone Community School in Grafton, Massachusetts. Her poems have appeared in *Something Understood* (from Every Other Thursday Press) and *Ad Hoc Monadnock.*

Ruth Buchman lives in Somerville, Massachusetts. Her poems have appeared in publications ranging from the *Antioch Review* to *Cricket.*

Claudia Buckholts has received fellowships from the National Endowment for the Arts (1988) and the Massachusetts Artists Foundation (1980). She is the author of two books of poems, *Bitterwater* (River House Press, 1975) and *Traveling through the Body* (Four Zoas Night House, 1979), and her poems have appeared in *Southern Poetry Review, Prairie Schooner, The Minnesota Review, Harvard Magazine,* and other journals.

Leslie Burgess earned a master's degree in fine arts from the University of Montana in 1983. She lives in Missoula, Montana, where she is a psychotherapist.

Carli Carrara retired from teaching elementary school and is focusing on becoming a better writer. A teacher/naturalist at the Moosehill Sanctuary in Sharon, Maine, she has had poems published in *Phoebe, Appalachia, Sojourner, Soundings East, Sandscript, Pebbles,* and *Passager* and has won various awards for her poems.

Naomi Feigelson Chase is the author of four books of poetry, *Stacked* (Garden Street Press, 1998), *Waiting for the Messiah in Somerville, Mass.* (Garden Street Press, 1993), *The Judge's Daughter* (Garden Street Press, 1996), and *Listening for Water* (Archival Press, 1980), as well as numerous short stories. She has recently won the Flume Press chapbook contest for *The One Blue Thread,* which will be published by California State University at Chico. She is also a founder of the Garden Street Press.

Eli Clare is a poet, essayist, rabble-rouser, and author of *Exile and Pride: Disability, Queerness, and Liberation* (South End Press, 1999).

Lynne Cohen is a librarian and digital video production teacher at Brookline High School in Brookline, Massachusetts. She also teaches at Cambridge College. Her poems have been published in *Sojourner* and

Free Lunch. She is coeditor of *Revisions: A Collection of Poems* (Talking Stone Press, 1998).

Martha Collins is Pauline Delaney Professor of Creative Writing at Oberlin College. She has published four books of poems, the most recent of which is *Some Things Words Can Do* (Sheep Meadow, 1999).

Elizabeth Crowell has an MFA degree in poetry from Columbia University. She writes and teaches in Massachusetts.

Cortney Davis, a nurse practitioner in women's health, is the author of two poetry collections, *Details of Flesh* (CALYX Books, 1997) and *The Body Flute* (Adastra Press, 1994), and a coeditor of two anthologies of writing by nurses, *Between the Heartbeats: Poetry and Prose by Nurses* (University of Iowa Press, 1995) and *Intensive Care* (University of Iowa Press, 2003). She has also written a memoir about her work with four female patients, *I Knew a Woman* (University of Iowa Press, 2001).

Carol Dine teaches English at Suffolk University in Boston. She received the 2001 Frances Locke Memorial Poetry Award from the Bitter Oleander Press for a poem from her series based on Vincent van Gogh. Her essay "The Layers" appears in the anthology *To Mend the World: Women Reflect on 9/11* (White Pine, 2002).

Rita Dove is Commonwealth Professor of English at the University of Virginia and served as U.S. Poet Laureate from 1993 to 1995. She has received numerous literary and academic honors, among them the 1987 Pulitzer Prize in Poetry, the 1996 National Humanities Medal, and the 2001 Duke Ellington Lifetime Achievement Award in the Literary Arts from the Ellington Fund in Washington, D.C.

Frances Driscoll is the author of a chapbook, *Talk to Me* (Black River, 1986), and *The Rape Poems* (Pleasureboat Studios, 1997). Her poem "Island of the Raped Women" won a Pushcart Prize, and eight other poems from *The Rape Poems* were Pushcart nominees. *Mudlark,* an electronic journal, published a chapbook issue from *The Rape Poems* in 1996.

Nancy Esposito is the recipient of a Discovery/The Nation Award, the Colladay Award, the Poetry Society of America Gordon Barber Memorial Award, a Fulbright Grant to Egypt in 1988, and Bentley College Faculty Development Grants for travel that included Vietnam and Cambodia. Her books of poems include *Changing Hands* (Quarterly Review of Literature Contemporary Poetry Series, 1984) and *Mêm' Rain* (Pudding

House Publications, 2002), winner of the National Looking Glass Poetry Chapbook Competition.

Liz Fenton has been a poetry editor at *Sojourner* and is the author of *Public Testimony* (Alice James Books, 1975). She does astrology and has translated various works of Theodore Rilke.

Caroline Finkelstein has been awarded grants from the states of Massachusetts and Vermont, is a two-time winner of the National Endowment for the Arts award for poetry, was an Amy Lowell Travelling Scholar for 1997–99, and most recently received the Mel Cohen Award at *Ploughshares.* She has published three collections of poetry; a fourth is forthcoming.

Janice Finney works for the Chicago Housing Authority Service Connector Program, which provides social services to public housing residents. Her poems have appeared in *Poetry East, Embers,* and *Oyez Review,* among other magazines, and "10 Pieces from a Horse Carcass" was displayed at Sterchis's in Chicago in collaboration with Owen Patrick Kerwin's paintings.

Sarah Fox, a teacher of poetry and creative writing, a letterpress publisher, and a doula, is the author of *Assembly of the Shades* (Salmon Press, 2003). She has received fellowships from the National Endowment for the Arts, the Bush Foundation, the Minnesota State Arts Board, and the Jerome Foundation.

Kathleen Fraser's most recent books of poems include *20th Century* (a+bend Press, 2000) and *Il cuore: The Heart—Selected Poems, 1970–1995* (Wesleyan University Press, 1997). She is also the author of *Translating the Unspeakable: Poetry and the Innovative Necessity* (University of Alabama Press, 2000), a collection of her essays.

Erica Funkhouser teaches introductory and advanced poetry writing workshops at MIT in Cambridge, Massachusetts. Her most recent book is *Pursuit* (Houghton Mifflin, 2002).

Kinereth Gensler, after teaching in the Radcliffe Seminars for many years, now teaches a poetry workshop in her home in Cambridge, Massachusetts. She has published three books of poetry with Alice James Books, the latest of which is *Journey Fruit* (1997). One of her essays appears in the collection *In Brief: Short Takes on the Personal* (W. W. Norton, 1999), and she had a poem published in the *Massachusetts Review.*

Celia Gilbert is a printmaker and poet in Cambridge, Massachusetts. The author of two books of poetry, *Bonfire* (Alice James Books, 1983) and *Queen of Darkness* (Viking, 1977), she received the first Jane Kenyon Chapbook Award for *An Ark of Sorts* (Alice James Books, 1998). Her poems have appeared in *Poetry, The New Yorker, Field,* and *Southwest Review,* among other journals.

Nikki Giovanni, University Distinguished Professor of English at Virginia Polytechnic Institute and State University, recently published an illustrated love poem titled *Knoxville, Tennessee* (Scholastic Trade; reprint ed., 1994) for her grandmother. Her other publications include *The Selected Poems of Nikki Giovanni: 1968–1995* (William Morrow and Co., 1996), *The Love Poems of Nikki Giovanni* (William Morrow and Co,, 1997), and *Blues: For All the Changes* (William Morrow and Co., 1999). She is also the editor of the anthologies *Grand/Mothers* (Henry Holt and Co., 1994) and *Grand/Fathers* (Henry Holt and Co., 1999). In April 2002 she was awarded the first Rosa L. Parks Woman of Courage Award.

Beckian Fritz Goldberg teaches in the creative writing program at Arizona State University. Her volumes of poetry include *Body Betrayer* (Cleveland State University Press, 1991), *In the Badlands of Desire* (Cleveland State University Press, 1993), *Never Be the Horse* (University of Akron Press, 1999), and the forthcoming *The Book of Accident* (University of Akron Press), and the chapbook *Twentieth-Century Children* (Graphic Design Press, 1999).

Stephanie Goldstein works in the Special Needs Program at Canton High School in Canton, Massachusetts. Her writing has been published by *The Senior Times* and *The Larcom Review.*

Miriam Goodman is the author of *Commercial Traveller* (Garden Street Press, 1996), *Signal::Noise* (Alice James Books, 1982), and *Permanent Wave* (Alice James Books, 1978) and the editor of an anthology of poetry on work for the electronic magazine *www.frigatezine.com* (no. 2). She lives in Somerville, Massachusetts, and has two daughters and two grandchildren.

Valerie Graham lives and works in Charlotte, Vermont. She is an active potter with a background in medical practice, town government, and arts education.

Anne Haines lives and works in Bloomington, Idaho. Her poems have previously appeared in a number of feminist and literary journals. She is at work on a book-length manuscript, tentatively titled "Land Mammal."

Vanessa Haley, formerly an associate professor of English at Mary Washington College, is a licensed clinical social worker in a private group practice in Wilmington, Delaware.

Marie Harris, the New Hampshire Poet Laureate for 1999–2004, is the author of *Your Sun, Manny: A Prose Poem Memoir* (New Rivers Press, 1999) and *G Is for Granite: A New Hampshire Alphabet* (Sleeping Bear Press, 2003).

Lola Haskins is the author of six books of poetry including *The Rim Benders* (Anhinga, 2001) and *Desire Lines: New and Selected* (BOA, forthcoming in 2004). Her work has also appeared in *The Atlantic, Georgia Review, Southern Review,* and other journals.

Lyn Hejinian teaches at the University of California at Berkeley. Her books include *Slowly* (Tuumba Press, 2002), *The Language of Inquiry* (University of California Press, 2000), a collection of essays, and *A Border Comedy* (Granary Books, 2001), among many others.

Jan Heller Levi lives in New York City and St. Gallen, Switzerland. She received the 1998 Walt Whitman Award of the Academy of American Poets for her first collection of poems, *Once I Gazed at You in Wonder* (Louisiana State University Press, 1999).

Fanny Howe is the author of *Selected Poems* (University of California Press, 2000) and *Indivisible (Native Agents)* (Semiotext/MIT Press, 2000), among many other novels and collections of poems.

Lynne Hugo lives in southwestern Ohio and has her own Web site, <http://www.lynnehugo.com>. She is the author of two collections of poetry, *The Time Change* (Ampersand Press, 1992) and *A Progress of Miracles* (San Diego Poets Press, 1993), and coauthor with Anna Tuttle Villegas of two novels, *Swimming Lessons* (William Morrow and Co., 1998) and *Baby's Breath* (Synergistic Press, 2000).

Julie Kalendek works in a plant nursery. Her most recent book is *Our Fortunes* (Burning Deck Press, 2003).

Kathryn Kirkpatrick teaches poetry and women's studies at Appalachian State University. Her books of poetry are *The Body's Horizon* (Signal Books, 1996), chosen by Alicia Ostriker for the Brockman-Campbell

Award, and *Beyond Reason* (Pecan Grove Press, 2003). She is the editor of *Cold Mountain Review* (<http://www.coldmountain.appstate.edu>).

Stephanie Koufman, a Boston-based painter and poet, is also a youth worker, focusing on teens through running after-school programs, coaching, and refereeing sports.

Ruth Lepson, poet-in-residence at the New England Conservatory of Music and adjunct faculty at the Art Institute of Boston at Lesley University, has organized poetry readings for Oxfam America and taught in the Massachusetts Poets-in-the-Schools Program. She is the author of *Dreaming in Color* (Alice James Books, 1980) and a book of dream prose poems, to be published by Potes & Poets Press in 2004. Her poems have appeared in *Agni, Ploughshares, The Women's Review of Books,* and many other journals.

Denise Levertov, a mentor to many and one of our finest poets, lived in Seattle for eight or nine years before her death in December 1997 from complications of lymphoma. Her last book of new poems was *Sands of the Well* (Bloodaxe Books Ltd., 1998). New Directions Press released *The Life around Us* and *The Stream and the Sapphire,* selections from her earlier books, shortly before she died.

Lyn Lifshin is the author *Before It's Light* (Black Sparrow Press, 1999), winner of the Paterson Poetry Award, and *Another Woman Who Looks Like Me* (Black Sparrow Books/David Godine, forthcoming). Her Web site is <http://www.lynlifshin.com>.

Margo Lockwood, a native of Boston, has retired from the secondhand bookshop featured in her poems. She is the author of *Three Poems Written in Ireland* (Menhaden Press, 1977), *Eight Poems* (Stationarius, 1981), *Bare Elegy* (Janus Press, 1980); *Temper* (Alice James Books, 1979), *Black Dog* (Alice James Books, 1986), and *Left-Handed Happiness* (Dirty Dish Press, 1989).

Mary Loeffelholz is chair of the Department of English at Northeastern University and the author of *Dickinson and the Boundaries of Feminist Theory* (University of Illinois Press, 1991) and *Experimental Lives: Women and Literature, 1900–1945* (Twayne/MacMillan, 1992). A book on nineteenth-century American women's poetry will be published by Princeton University Press.

Audre Lorde was an acclaimed social activist, professor of English at John Jay College of Criminal Justice and at Hunter College, and New York

State Poet from 1991 to 1993. She published nine volumes of poetry and five works of prose and was the recipient of many distinguished honors and awards, including the Walt Whitman Citation of Merit, the Manhattan Borough President's Award for Excellence in the Arts, and the American Book Award. A cancer survivor for many years, she succumbed to the disease in 1992 on the island of St. Croix, West Indies.

Ruth Maassen, the author of *Picking Raspberries* (Folly Cove Books, 1997), is working on her first novel.

Michelle M. Maihiot lives in Dublin, New Hampshire, with "the cutest woman in the world and their genius cats." Her work has appeared in *Midwest Poetry Review* and *The Rockford Review,* among other journals.

Jennifer Markell lives in the Boston area and works as a child-family therapist and urban gardener who tends children, flowers, and poems. She was a special merit finalist in the *Comstock Review*'s annual poetry competition (2000) and received a commendation in the Chester H. Jones Foundation poetry competition in 1996. Her poems have been published in *Bridges Journal, Carapace,* and *Talking River Review.*

Suzanne Matson, a professor at Boston College, lives in Newton, Massachusetts, with her husband and three young sons. She is the author of two books of poems, *Sea Level* (1990) and *Durable Goods* (1993), both from Alice James Books, and two novels, *The Hunger Moon* (1997) and *A Trick of Nature* (2000), both from W. W. Norton.

Linda McCarriston lives in Bear Valley, Alaska, along with several animals collectively known as the "Musicians of Bremen." She teaches in the MFA program at the University of Alaska at Anchorage, where her students have been enjoying success during and following their apprenticeships. Her recent books, *Eva-Mary* (1991) and *Little River* (2002), were published by Northwestern University Press.

Helena Minton, whose poems have appeared in *The Acre* and *The Larcom Review,* works in a public library in Massachusetts. She is a coauthor, with Robin Becker and Marilyn Zuckerman, of *Personal Effects* (1976) and the author of *The Canal Bed* (1985), both published by Alice James Books.

Honor Moore teaches in the graduate writing programs at Columbia University and The New School. Her most recent collection is *Darling* (Grove, 2001), and she is also the author of *The White Blackbird* (Viking and Penguin, 1996 and 1997), about her grandmother, the painter Margarett Sargent.

Rosario Morales spends her mornings writing fiction, memoir, and—sometimes—poetry; the rest of her time is dedicated to friends, family, husband, home, books, and garden. She coauthored *Getting Home Alive* (Firebrand Books, 1986) with her daughter Aurora Levins Morales, and her work has also appeared in the anthology *This Bridge Called My Back* (Kitchen Table/Women of Color, 1989) and the journals *Sojourner* and *Callaloo,* among other publications.

Robin Morgan, an award-winning poet, novelist, political theorist, journalist, and editor, has published seventeen books. A founder/leader of contemporary U.S. feminism, she has also been a leader in the international women's movement for twenty-five years.

Kate Mullen lives just outside Boston, Massachusetts, and is employed as a dance instructor. A graduate of Northeastern University, she writes poetry and, as a freelance writer, has contributed articles to several newspapers.

Nina Nyhart is married and lives in Brookline, Massachusetts. Her poems have been published widely, and she has two collections of poetry from Alice James Books, *Openers* (1979) and *French for Soldiers* (1987). She also coauthored, with Kinereth Gensler, *The Poetry Connection* (Teachers and Writers Collaborative, 1978), a text for teachers and students.

Dzvinia Orlowsky, a founding editor of Four Way Books, is a member of the MFA poetry faculty at Stonecoast, University of Southern Maine. Her third collection of poetry is *Except for One Obscene Brushstroke* (Carnegie Mellon University Press, 2003).

Molly Peacock, poet-in-residence at the Cathedral of St. John the Divine, is the author of *Cornucopia: New and Selected Poems 1975–2002* (W. W. Norton/Penguin Canada, 2002), *How to Read a Poem—and Start a Poetry Circle* (McClelland and Stewart, 1999), and a memoir, *Paradise, Piece by Piece* (Riverhead Books, 1998), among other books. She also edited *The Private I: Privacy in a Public World* (Graywolf Press, 2001) for the Graywolf Forum 2001.

Joyce Peseroff is a visiting professor and poet-in-residence at the University of Massachusetts at Boston. Her three books of poems are *The Hardness Scale* (Alice James Books, 1977), *A Dog in the Lifeboat* (Carnegie Mellon, 1991), and *Mortal Education* (Carnegie Mellon 2000). She is also the editor of *Robert Bly: When Sleepers Awake* (University of Michigan Press, 1984) and *The Ploughshares Poetry Reader* (Ploughshares Books/New American Library, 1984).

Carol Potter teaches at Antioch University in Los Angeles and is a 2001 recipient of a Pushcart Prize. She has published three books of poems, the most recent being *Short History of Pets* (2000), winner of the Cleveland State University Poetry Center Award and the Balcones Award.

Martha Ramsey lives in Vermont and is the author of *Where I Stopped: Remembering Rape at Thirteen* (Putnam, 1995; Harvest 1997), a memoir, and *Blood Stories* (Cleveland State University Poetry Series, 1996).

Jane Ransom is the author of a novel, *Bye-Bye* (1997), which won the New York University Press Prize for Fiction, and two books of poems, *Scene of the Crime* (Story Line Press, 1997) and *Without Asking* (Story Line Press, 1989), which won the Nicholas Roerich Prize.

Mary Kathleen Rayburn, reared in Indiana and a former Bostonian, now lives and writes in Santa Barbara, California.

Monica Raymond, a poet and playwright, is fixing up an old house in Cambridge, Massachusetts.

Elizabeth Rees is a poet-in-the-schools for the Maryland State Arts Council. Her poems have appeared in *Agni, Partisan Review,* and *Kenyon Review,* among other journals.

Rita Mae Reese won the Dean's Prize in creative writing at Florida State University and is now a Martha Meier Rank Fellow at the University of Wisconsin at Madison. Two of her poems won 2001–2002 Associated Writing Program Intro Journals Project awards and have appeared in *Shenandoah* and *Mid-America Review.*

Adrienne Rich, a resident of California since 1984, has published more than fifteen volumes of poetry, most recently *Fox: Poems 1998–2000* (W. W. Norton and Company, 2003).

Mary Susannah Robbins, who operates an editorial service, is the editor of *Against the Vietnam War: Writings by Activists* (Syracuse University Press, 1999) and the author of *Amelie* (Ommation Press, 1986). Her etchings, monoprints, and monotypes can be found in collections all over the world and are in the collections of the Fogg Museum, the Smith College Museum of Art, and the Loeb Art Center at Vassar College.

Jennifer Rose, the recipient of awards from the National Endowment for the Arts and other organizations, lives in Waltham, Massachusetts, and works as a city planner specializing in the revitalization of urban commercial districts. She is the author of *The Old Direction of Heaven* (Truman State University Press, 2000), and her poems have appeared in *Ploughshares, Poetry, The Nation,* and elsewhere.

Ellen A. Rosen received her MFA in writing from the School of the Art Institute of Chicago in 2001 and is currently employed as a writing specialist at Ariel Community Academy, a Chicago public school. Her poetry has appeared in many literary journals, including *Rhino, Iris, Columbia Poetry Review,* and *New American Writing.*

Mariève Rugo is the author of *Fields of Vision* (University of Alabama Press, 1983) and has spent most of the past five years writing a memoir, currently titled "Perfection." Her poems have appeared in the *Kenyon Review, Southern Review, Quarterly West,* and *Seneca Review,* among other journals.

Kate Rushin has served on the faculty of the Cave Canem New York Poetry Workshop at Poets House and teaches poetry workshops and courses on black writers in the African American Studies Program at Wesleyan University. She is the author of "The Bridge Poem" and two books of poetry, *The Black Back-ups* (Firebrand Books, 1993) and *Camden Sweet, Lawnside Blues.*

Sonia Sanchez, who has lectured at more than five hundred universities and colleges and read her poetry worldwide, is the recipient of many honors and awards, including the 1985 American Book Award for *Homegirls and Handgrenades* (1985) and the Poetry Society of America's 2001 Robert Frost Medal. She is the author of more than sixteen books, including *Wounded in the House of a Friend* (Beacon Press, 1995), *Does Your House Have Lions?* (Beacon Press, 1997), and *Shake Loose My Skin* (Beacon Press, 1999).

Cheryl Savageau has been awarded fellowships from the National Endowment for the Arts and the Massachusetts Artists Foundation. In 1996 she received a Writer of the Year Award from Wordcraft Circle of the Native Writers and Storytellers for her children's book *Muskrat Will Be Swimming* (Northland Publishing Co., 1996), which was also named a Notable Book by *Smithsonian* magazine. Her second book of poetry, *Dirt Road Home* (Curbstone Press, 1995), was nominated for a Pulitzer Prize and was a finalist for the 1996 Patterson Prize.

Leslie Scalapino, publisher of O Books, is the author of *Defoe* (reprinted by Green Integer, 2002), *The Tango* (Granary Books, 2001), *New Time* (Wesleyan University Press, 1999), *The Return of Painting, The Pearl, and Orion: A Trilogy* (North Point Press, 1991), *Green and Black: Selected Writing* (Talisman House, 1996), and *The Front Matter, Dead Souls* (Wesleyan University Press, 1996), and many other books of poetry, fiction, plays, and essays. *The Return of Painting* has been reprinted by Talisman.

Betsy Sholl lives in Portland, Maine, and teaches at the University of Southern Maine and in the MFA program at Vermont College. Her most recent books are *Don't Explain* (University of Wisconsin Press, 1997) and *The Red Line* (University of Pittsburgh Press, 1992).

Beverly Jean Smith, former chair of the *Harvard Educational Review,* is an assistant professor of education at Leslie University. Her poetry has appeared in *Sojourner* and *An Ear to the Ground* (University of Georgia Press, 1989).

Ann Spanel, an artist, activist, and poet, lives with a cat and enjoys the skunks, bees, slugs, worms, squirrels, birds, and spirits who inhabit her garden.

Kathleen Spivack teaches in Paris and Boston and gives performances, readings, and workshops worldwide. She has published six books of poetry and prose.

Judith W. Steinbergh, the recipient of a Wordworks' Washington Prize and a Bunting Institute fellow at Radcliffe College, has taught poetry and writing in the Boston area for more than thirty years. Her most recent collection is *Writing My Will* (Talking Stone Press, 2001).

Mary Louise Sullivan, nominated as a PEN/New England "Discovery" novelist for *The Sound of a Half Moon,* lives in Cambridge, Massachusetts, and Martha's Vineyard, where she continues to write poetry and fiction.

Kate Taylor, a poet and writer, has been employed as a bicycle mechanic, farmer, editor, and mental health worker before settling down as a furniture maker. Her work has appeared in journals ranging from *Jugglers World* to *Sinister Wisdom.*

Lee Varon, a past poetry editor at *Sojourner,* writes short stories and poetry.

Cornelia Veenendaal is the author of three volumes of poetry and is working on two more. Her poems have appeared in *Frigatezine, Hanging Loose, The Larcom Review,* and *Yankee,* among other publications.

Rosmarie Waldrop is the author of *Reluctant Gravities* (New Directions, 1999), *Split Infinites* (Singing Horse Press, 1998), *Another Language: Selected Poems* (Talisman House, 1997), and many other books. Her two novels, *The Hanky of Pippin's Daughter* and *A Form/of Taking/It All* were reprinted in one volume by Northwestern University Press in 2001.

Lynne Weiss lives in the Boston area, where she works as a writer and editor. She has completed her first novel, titled "Singing for Jack."

Jeanne Wells lives on the Maine coast, where she works as a bookseller. Her essays, poems, and fiction have appeared in various publications, including *Blackfly Review, Beliot Poetry Journal,* and *f/m,* a publication of the Women's Education Research and Resource Centre, University College, Dublin.

Ruth Whitman wrote several narrative poems about the lives of extraordinary women, including the murderess Lizzie Borden (1963), the pioneer Tamsen Donner (1966), the Israeli parachutist Hanna Senesh (1968), the pharoah Hatshepsut (1993), and Isadora Duncan, the inventor of modern dance. Her aim was to get under the skin of these women and write from their point of view, focusing at the same time on what was so extraordinary about them.

Lee Whitman-Raymond holds master's degrees in fine arts and social work and is a doctoral candidate in and adjunct faculty member of the Simmons College School for Social Work. The recipient of a University Prize from the American Academy of Poets, she has just published a chapbook of poems, *The Light on Our Faces: A Therapy Dialogue* (Pleasureboat Studios, 2000). Her poems have also appeared in the *Worcester Review, Northeast Journal, Sandscript, Brown Journal, Kaleidoscope,* and other publications.

Louise Grassi Whitney, born and raised on the East Coast, has lived in California for many years. In 1991 she placed her autistic son in a group home and began writing poetry to cope with the changes. Her poems has been widely published and included in several anthologies.

Carla Willard, an associate professor of American and Africana Studies at Franklin and Marshall College, lives in Philadelphia with her inspiring husband and three nephews. Her poems have appeared in major reviews and journals, and she is working on a book of poetry as well as a monograph on the rise of national media in the United States

Jeanette I. Winthrop, a retired teacher who taught first-grade reading, started writing when she turned fifty and joined a poetry workshop.

S. L. Wisenberg lives in Chicago, where she works as a teacher and writing coach. The author of a book of stories, *The Sweetheart Is In* (Northwestern University Press, 2001), and an essay collection, *Holocaust Girls: History, Memory, and Other Obsessions* (University of Nebraska Press, 2002), she has her own Web site at <http://www.slwisenberg.com>.

Francine Witte lives in New York City and teaches creative writing in the public school system. Her one-act plays have been performed on New York's Theatre Row and her poems have appeared in *Tar River Poetry, Cream City Review, Calliope, Skylark,* and other publications. She is the author of a chapbook, *The Magic in the Streets* (Owl Creek Press, 1994).

Nancy Means Wright lives, writes, and teaches in Vermont. She is the author of ten books of fiction and poetry, most recently *Stolen Honey* (St. Martin's Press, 2002). Her poems have appeared in anthologies published by Beacon Press, St. Martin's, and Ashland Poetry Press, among others.

Lynne Yamaguchi was a poetry editor at *Sojourner* from 1992 to 1995. She coedited the anthology *Tomboys! Tales of Dyke Derring-do* (Alyson, 1995) with Karen Barber, and her poetry, essays, and erotica have been published in periodicals and anthologies including *Close Calls, Lesbian Culture, She Who Was Lost Is Remembered,* and *The Forbidden Stitch.*

Robyn Zappala lives in Burlington, Vermont, and is a fervent Kim and Kerry fan.

Rosamond Zimmermann lives and writes in Lexington, Massachusetts.

Marilyn Zuckerman, the recipient of a PEN Syndicated Fiction Award and an Allen Ginsberg Poetry Award, is the author of *Personal Effects* (Alice James Books, 1976), *Monday Morning Movie* (Street Editions, 1981), *Poems of the Sixth Decade* (Garden Street Press, 1993), and *Amerika/America* (Cedar Hill Publications, 2002), as well as the chapbook *Greatest Hits 1970–2000* (2002) in the Pudding House Publications series The Greatest Hits.

Martha Zweig has been a feminist, a revolutionary, a single mother, a garment factory worker, and an advocate for the elderly and women surviving abuse. Her poems have appeared widely, including in *Fine Madness, Black Warrior Review, Nimrod, Boston Review, American Voice, Kenyon Review,* and *Northwest Review.*

Editors' Note: A small number of the poets we contacted did not respond to our request for updated biographical information. In these few cases, we relied on information provided earlier in the process of putting together this anthology.

Index of Titles

Illinois Poetry Series
Laurence Lieberman, Editor

History Is Your Own Heartbeat
Michael S. Harper (1971)

The Foreclosure
Richard Emil Braun (1972)

The Scrawny Sonnets and Other
Narratives
Robert Bagg (1973)

The Creation Frame
Phyllis Thompson (1973)

To All Appearances: Poems New and
Selected
Josephine Miles (1974)

The Black Hawk Songs
Michael Borich (1975)

Nightmare Begins Responsibility
Michael S. Harper (1975)

The Wichita Poems
Michael Van Walleghen (1975)

Images of Kin: New and
Selected Poems
Michael S. Harper (1977)

Poems of the Two Worlds
Frederick Morgan (1977)

Cumberland Station
Dave Smith (1977)

Tracking
Virginia R. Terris (1977)

Riversongs
Michael Anania (1978)

On Earth as It Is
Dan Masterson (1978)

Coming to Terms
Josephine Miles (1979)

Death Mother and Other Poems
Frederick Morgan (1979)

Goshawk, Antelope
Dave Smith (1979)

Local Men
James Whitehead (1979)

Searching the Drowned Man
Sydney Lea (1980)

With Akhmatova at the Black Gates
Stephen Berg (1981)

Dream Flights
Dave Smith (1981)

More Trouble with the Obvious
Michael Van Walleghen (1981)

The American Book of the Dead
Jim Barnes (1982)

The Floating Candles
Sydney Lea (1982)

Northbook
Frederick Morgan (1982)

Collected Poems, 1930–83
Josephine Miles (1983; reissue, 1999)

The River Painter
Emily Grosholz (1984)

Healing Song for the Inner Ear
Michael S. Harper (1984)

The Passion of the Right-Angled Man
T. R. Hummer (1984)

Dear John, Dear Coltrane
Michael S. Harper (1985)

Poems from the Sangamon
John Knoepfle (1985)

In It
Stephen Berg (1986)

The Ghosts of Who We Were
Phyllis Thompson (1986)

Moon in a Mason Jar
Robert Wrigley (1986)

Lower-Class Heresy
T. R. Hummer (1987)

Poems: New and Selected
Frederick Morgan (1987)

Furnace Harbor: A Rhapsody of the
North Country
Philip D. Church (1988)

Bad Girl, with Hawk
Nance Van Winckel (1988)

Blue Tango
Michael Van Walleghen (1989)

Eden
Dennis Schmitz (1989)

Waiting for Poppa at the Smithtown
Diner
Peter Serchuk (1990)

Great Blue
Brendan Galvin (1990)

What My Father Believed
Robert Wrigley (1991)

Something Grazes Our Hair
S. J. Marks (1991)

Walking the Blind Dog
G. E. Murray (1992)

The Sawdust War
Jim Barnes (1992)

The God of Indeterminacy
Sandra McPherson (1993)

Off-Season at the Edge of the World
Debora Greger (1994)

Counting the Black Angels
Len Roberts (1994)

Oblivion
Stephen Berg (1995)

To Us, All Flowers Are Roses
Lorna Goodison (1995)

Honorable Amendments
Michael S. Harper (1995)

Points of Departure
Miller Williams (1995)

Dance Script with Electric Ballerina
Alice Fulton (reissue, 1996)

To the Bone: New and Selected Poems
Sydney Lea (1996)

Floating on Solitude
Dave Smith (3-volume reissue, 1996)

Bruised Paradise
Kevin Stein (1996)

Walt Whitman Bathing
David Wagoner (1996)

Rough Cut
Thomas Swiss (1997)

Paris
Jim Barnes (1997)

The Ways We Touch
Miller Williams (1997)

The Rooster Mask
Henry Hart (1998)

The Trouble-Making Finch
Len Roberts (1998)

Grazing
Ira Sadoff (1998)

Turn Thanks
Lorna Goodison (1999)

Traveling Light:
Collected and New Poems
David Wagoner (1999)

Some Jazz a While:
Collected Poems
Miller Williams (1999)

The Iron City
John Bensko (2000)

Songlines in Michaeltree: New and
Collected Poems
Michael S. Harper (2000)

Pursuit of a Wound
Sydney Lea (2000)

The Pebble: Old and New Poems
Mairi MacInnes (2000)

Chance Ransom
Kevin Stein (2000)

House of Poured-Out Waters
Jane Mead (2001)

The Silent Singer: New and Selected
Poems
Len Roberts (2001)

The Salt Hour
J. P. White (2001)

Guide to the Blue Tongue
Virgil Suárez (2002)

The House of Song
David Wagoner (2002)

X =
Stephen Berg (2002)

Arts of a Cold Sun
G. E. Murray (2003)

Barter
Ira Sadoff (2003)

The Hollow Log Lounge
R. T. Smith (2003)

National Poetry Series

Eroding Witness
Nathaniel Mackey (1985)
Selected by Michael S. Harper

Palladium
Alice Fulton (1986)
Selected by Mark Strand

Cities in Motion
Sylvia Moss (1987)
Selected by Derek Walcott

The Hand of God and a Few
Bright Flowers
William Olsen (1988)
Selected by David Wagoner

The Great Bird of Love
Paul Zimmer (1989)
Selected by William Stafford

Stubborn
Roland Flint (1990)
Selected by Dave Smith

The Surface
Laura Mullen (1991)
Selected by C. K. Williams

The Dig
Lynn Emanuel (1992)
Selected by Gerald Stern

My Alexandria
Mark Doty (1993)
Selected by Philip Levine

The High Road to Taos
Martin Edmunds (1994)
Selected by Donald Hall

Theater of Animals
Samn Stockwell (1995)
Selected by Louise Glück

The Broken World
Marcus Cafagña (1996)
Selected by Yusef Komunyakaa

Nine Skies
A. V. Christie (1997)
Selected by Sandra McPherson

Lost Wax
Heather Ramsdell (1998)
Selected by James Tate

So Often the Pitcher Goes to Water
until It Breaks
Rigoberto González (1999)
Selected by Ai

Renunciation
Corey Marks (2000)
Selected by Philip Levine

Manderley
Rebecca Wolff (2001)
Selected by Robert Pinsky

Theory of Devolution
David Groff (2002)
Selected by Mark Doty

Rhythm and Booze
Julie Kane (2003)
Selected by Maxine Kumin

Other Poetry Volumes

Local Men and *Domains*
James Whitehead (1987)

Her Soul beneath the Bone: Women's
Poetry on Breast Cancer
Edited by Leatrice Lifshitz (1988)

Days from a Dream Almanac
Dennis Tedlock (1990)

Working Classics: Poems on Industrial
Life
*Edited by Peter Oresick and Nicholas
Coles* (1990)

Hummers, Knucklers, and Slow
Curves: Contemporary Baseball
Poems
Edited by Don Johnson (1991)

The Double Reckoning of Christopher
Columbus
Barbara Helfgott Hyett (1992)

Selected Poems
Jean Garrigue (1992)

New and Selected Poems, 1962–92
Laurence Lieberman (1993)

The Dig and *Hotel Fiesta*
Lynn Emanuel (1994)

For a Living: The Poetry of Work
Edited by Nicholas Coles and Peter
Oresick (1995)

The Tracks We Leave: Poems on
Endangered Wildlife of North
America
Barbara Helfgott Hyett (1996)

Peasants Wake for Fellini's *Casanova*
and Other Poems
Andrea Zanzotto; edited and translated
by John P. Welle and Ruth Feldman;
drawings by Federico Fellini and
Augusto Murer (1997)

Moon in a Mason Jar and *What My*
Father Believed
Robert Wrigley (1997)

The Wild Card: Selected Poems, Early
and Late
Karl Shapiro; edited by Stanley Kunitz
and David Ignatow (1998)

Turtle, Swan and *Bethlehem in Broad*
Daylight
Mark Doty (2000)

Illinois Voices: An Anthology of
Twentieth-Century Poetry
Edited by Kevin Stein and G. E. Murray
(2001)

On a Wing of the Sun
Jim Barnes (3-volume reissue, 2001)

Poems
William Carlos Williams; introduction
by Virginia M. Wright-Peterson (2002)

Creole Echoes: The Francophone
Poetry of Nineteenth-Century
Louisiana
Translated by Norman R. Shapiro;
introduction and notes by M. Lynn
Weiss (2003)

Poetry from *Sojourner:* A Feminist
Anthology
Edited by Ruth Lepson with Lynne
Yamaguchi; introduction by Mary
Loeffelholz (2003)

The University of Illinois Press
is a founding member of the
Association of American University Presses.

Composed in 10.5/13 Minion
with Centaur Italic display
by Celia Shapland
for the University of Illinois Press
Designed by Dennis Roberts
Manufactured by Sheridan Books, Inc.

University of Illinois Press
1325 South Oak Street
Champaign, IL 61820-6903
www.press.uillinois.edu